Classic Motorbooks

CHEVY EL CAMINO 1959-1982

Photofacts

DONALD F. WOOD

Motorbooks International
Publishers & Wholesalers Inc.
Osceola, Wisconsin 54020, USA

ISBN: 0-87938-136-1
Library of Congress Number: 81-22554

Printed and bound in the United States of America. Book and cover design by William F. Kosfeld.

2 3 4 5 6 7 8 9 10

Front cover photo courtesy of Mr. Loren Eickhoff.

Library of Congress Cataloging in Publication Data

Wood, Donald F.
Chevrolet El Camino 1959-1982.

(Classic motorbooks photofacts)
1. El Camino automobile. I. Title.
II. Series.
TL215.C335W66 629.2'222 81-22554
ISBN 0-87938-136-1 (pbk.) AACR2

To Professor James C. Johnson
of St. Cloud State University

PREFACE

Writing a book about Chevrolet El Caminos was a challenge because, in one sense, the vehicle is neither a car nor a truck. I decided to avoid that approach, and did not dwell long upon what the El Camino *is not*. Instead, I concentrated upon what the El Camino—and its cousins, the Sprint and Caballero—are: versatile vehicles which give to many owners the best of both worlds! I also tried to avoid compiling a *trivia* book and, rather than repeat voluminous, and often repetitive, data for each year, I refer individuals interested in a specific year El Camino to purchase literature issued for that year's model. Where facts and changes are mentioned in this book, it is for the purpose of tracing the El Camino's evolution.

Many people have helped with this book and I hope that I have named them all here. I regret that most of them are known to me only by mail or long-distance phone. They are, of course, not responsible for any errors the book may contain.

Thanks go to: Randy Aaronian; Howard and Shelby Applegate; Donald Bougher, Light Commercial Vehicle Association; Ed Breslin, Chevrolet Motor Division; Morley Brown; Michael Bryant; Roger M. Callies; Jeff Carr; J. D. Castor; Robert Cerame; Fred W. Chel, Custom Hardtops; Sophia Cortez, Protect-O-Top; B. H. Craig; Dallas Area Classic Chevys Club; Tomm Davis; Ricky Darling; Gary DaVanzo; Kermit Debban; Dennis Doty; Luvern Eickhoff; Dan Frank; Bill Franson; Jerry Gentry; Mike Gulden; David Harriman; Milt Hill; Gary E. Hinkle, Auto-West Advertising; Larry Kasson; Tony Kemp; Gordon W. King; Mike Lambert; Michael Lamm; "Skip" Lecates; Mark Lenhardt; Chuck Licari, GMC Truck and Coach Division; Daniel Logan, Bearcat Corporation; Bill Luke; Todd Martin; Carl Matson, Chevrolet Motor Division; Sherman Mehloff; Robert Merrifield, Sr.; Mark Mitchell; Mike Moore, Harrah's Automobile Collection; David Moraca; Albert T. Olson, Jr., Chevrolet Motor Division; Tony Palmasano; Roger Pardue; Pete Pesterre, *Popular Hot Rodding;* Bart Rawson, American Truck Historical Society; Margaretta Sandula, Detroit Public Library; Kelvin Schott; L. Schwartz, Lindberg Products, Inc.; Larry Seidel; Lewis Shaw; Will Sibbald; Jim Slavic; R. Scott Smyers; Kevin Stamps; Ken Stang; Steve Stefinsky; Randy Stickelman; Lee C. Stockland, The Stockland Company; Marc Struglia; John W. Sturgis, Ayr-way Industries; Bob Wingate, Bob Wingate's Classics; Larry Trask; Royal Waldock; Rick Waldorf, Monogram Models; Jeannie Whitehead; Dan Willis, Gem Top Manufacturing; Bob Woolley, *Model Car Journal;* John Yates; and Keith Zimmerman.

I also want to thank William Kosfeld and Barbara Harold at Motorbooks International for their encouragement and assistance, and for turning envelopes of typewritten pages and photos into this book!

Donald F. Wood
San Francisco State University

A NOTE ABOUT 'AUTHENTIC' PICTURES

Some readers will be interested in knowing exactly what a specific El Camino or Sprint/Caballero model should look like. Many of the photos appearing in this book are of vehicles which have been "customized" or modified slightly. Photos with either the Chevrolet or GMC credit line are the most original.

Photos without a factory credit line may or may not show the vehicle as originally manufactured. When customizing is described, there is a chance that some details were overlooked.

Many pictures I took were views from the vehicles' rear, which makes it difficult to specify a year, since the only changes were in the front. These photos are placed approximately where they belong in model sequence, although the exact model year is not specified in the caption. (If readers detect errors in vehicle identification—or elsewhere in the text—they should write to the author, in care of the publisher.)

CONTENTS

INTRODUCTION

The Chevrolet El Camino functions as both an auto and a truck. This should not be considered unusual; all passenger automobiles have a varying ability to carry freight, and trucks also carry passengers. (Some trucks even have "crew" cabs, with full front and back seats.)

A listing of all freight-carrying capabilities and features of autos would be exhaustive since virtually every year and body style would have to be included. Rather than do that, I have included a sample captioned photo showing one way in which autos were used to carry freight.

For many years, automobile manufacturers produced a "commercial" chassis, for which independent body builders would construct specialized bodies, including station wagon bodies. The auto manufacturers themselves sometimes used these chassis for their own lines of light trucks, including pickups and sedan deliveries. (See this author's article in *Special-Interest Autos,* #49, February, 1979.) Beginning about 1950, there was less use of the automobile commercial chassis. One reason for this decline was that the automobile's lower lines and the re-

From 1936 through 1942, Chevrolet offered a "coupe delivery" which was a pickup bed fitted into the standard coupe. (The box was removable and the trunk door could be reinstalled.' *(Baker Library, Harvard University)*

This 1938 Studebaker shared the same chassis and much of the body with the passenger car. *(Smithsonian Institution)*

quirements for streamlining reduced the vehicle's potential for carrying freight.

An Australian Ford of the 1930's, combining a roadster front and full pickup rear, nicknamed the Ute, is credited by James K. Wagner, in his *Ford Trucks Since 1905* (Glen Ellyn, IL: Crestline Publishing, 1978), and by John Gunnell, in *Old Cars Weekly* (January 15, 1981), as being the direct ancestor of the Ranchero/El Camino body type. Chevrolet also built its version of the Ute in Australia; see George H. Dammann's *Sixty Years of Chevrolet* (Glen Ellyn, IL: Crestline Publishing, 1972).

While the Ute looks like a fairly direct ancestor, it was not unique. Many other autos and light trucks produced in the United States could also claim to be a link in the process by which the El Camino/Ranchero body evolved.

Albert Olson, Jr., Chevrolet's assistant general sales manager who was involved with Chevrolet's initial introduction of the El Camino, said that the El Camino was brought out to meet a West Coast market need for a "comfortable" pickup. Potential users were expected to be ranch owners, oil field supervisors, etc.; individuals who felt that they should be driving a truck but wanted more comfort and style. A secondary market would be businesses that wanted a stylish pickup. Olson's specific example here was a Beverly Hills swimming pool maintenance service. The name "El Camino" was a favorite choice of the group developing the new vehicle, according to Olson, although they had to obtain permission from another division of GM, which had used it on an experimental auto. El Camino means approximately "road" or "highway" in Spanish. A historic road leading through California is named the "El Camino Real" (pronounced re-al). Olson said that "real" was not included in the vehicle's name because its pronunciation would only cause confusion.

Somewhat by accident, it was discovered that the El Camino's dual status (split personality?) as a car and a truck could work to its owner's advantage. Many states offered the choice of registering an El Camino as an auto or a truck. When registered as an auto it could operate as a truck in residential areas where trucks were prohibited. One owner told me that an advantage of owning an El Camino over a

Sedan deliveries used the automobile body. This is a 1954 Chevrolet. *(Motor Vehicle Manufacturers Association)*

Ford introduced the Ranchero, on a passenger-car-size chassis, in 1957. In 1960, the Ranchero was downsized to the Falcon chassis. A 1961 Ranchero is shown here. In the late 1960's, the Ranchero's size grew, as did the number and size of power options. Ford stopped building Rancheros in 1979.

conventional truck was that at drive-in movies, the El Caminos could mix in the lot with autos while the conventional pickups and vans were relegated to the back row of the lot.

When registered as a truck, the owner could—in some states—park in loading zones. More important was that the owner could insure his El Camino as a truck and enjoy lower rates; even if he were driving what he, and I, would consider to be a "muscle car." Some businessmen might prefer to call the vehicle a truck for tax purposes since a truck often would seem more necessary to a business (or farm).

In the course of writing this book, I surveyed owners of about seventy-five El Caminos with a number of questions, including one asking whether they registered their vehicle as an auto or a truck. Only one out of six registered the El Camino as an auto, the rest registered it as a truck. In a question about El Camino features the owners *disliked,* the answers reflected the sacrifices which must be made to achieve a combined auto/truck. There were complaints about the small size of the cab for carrying passengers (or accommodating stereo speakers), although this was not a unanimous feeling since one owner considered the small cab as an advantage because he didn't "have to haul other people around." Also, there were complaints about the vehicle's load-carrying capability. (The only other complaints dealt with rear window leaks, which are not unique to El Caminos.)

In preparing this book, one of the questions upon which I tried to focus was whether the El Camino was perceived as an auto or as a truck. One of the owners surveyed said, in effect: "It's a truck, dummy! Even the nameplate says so."

I asked Virginia Neto, the well-known California social scientist, and she responded that the owners "keep their El Caminos all polished and drive around seldom carrying anything in the back. . . . Of course, they're a car." In retrospect, too much time may have been spent worrying about whether the El Camino was an auto or a truck. Albert Olson, Jr., of Chevrolet solved the dilemma rather quickly by saying that the El Camino was whichever its owner wanted it to be.

In addition to being of value to their first-time buyers, some cars and trucks enjoy continued popularity and are desired by subsequent owners who attempt

Conventional pickups were also becoming stylish in the late '50's. This is a 1958 Chevrolet. *(Free Library of Philadelphia)*

to either restore them to their original condition or to "customize" them. In an attempt to determine whether El Caminos will achieve *collector* status, I interviewed Bob Wingate of Bob Wingate's Classics in San Dimas, California (a Los Angeles suburb). Bob specializes in the restoration, refurbishing and resale of older (ten-to-thirty years) Chevies. An article about Bob appeared in a 1981 issue of *The Wall Street Journal* referring to him as "the guru of the 1950's vintage Chevrolet." I asked him first to compare what he thought the market for used El Caminos was in comparison to used Chevrolet automobiles of similar vintage, and he said: "The popularity of the early El Caminos has already established itself firmly in the special interest automobile market. Nice, clean, original type El Caminos are harder to find than the comparable passenger vehicle. Most of them were 'run hard and put away wet.' Consequently the enthusiast has a difficult time finding a nice representative model."

I probed about the advantages and disadvantages of used El Caminos in comparison to conventional Chevrolet pickups, and Wingate said: "The main disadvantages of an El Camino over a conventional pickup are the difference in payload; the conventional pickup is designed to haul larger payloads. Also they have a corresponding ride. The pickup rides stiff and bouncy because of the suspension required to haul the payload.

"The advantages of an El Camino would be that it has the comforts of a car but still is a workhorse in that it can do some hauling. The styling characteristics have traditionally been more exciting on the El Camino."

Asked if he sold many Ford Rancheros, Bob said, "Ford Rancheros have sold well but we do not see the interest or enthusiasm in them like we do in the El Caminos. That is not to take anything away from the Rancheros because they are a fine vehicle and they were first (1957) in producing this type of vehicle in America." And he made these comparisons between El Caminos and Rancheros: "The El Caminos seem to enjoy more flexibility in their ability to interchange mechanical parts longer than the Rancheros. One of the concerns of customers is how economical a vehicle is going to be to operate, so the interchangeability is frequently discussed. Minor driving characteristics, peculiar to each model, do not hinder a buying decision for either of the two vehicles."

I concluded by asking whether he thought El Caminos were on their way toward becoming a collector car, and Wingate said he believed that "the El Caminos are well on the road to being a collector vehicle. They are very versatile and having a two-fold purpose appeal to a wide range of people. The El Camino has excellent styling and is just a downright good looking piece of equipment. One added bonus feature now is that the price on these fun machines is quite reasonable compared to other comparable cars. That doesn't hurt too many feelings!"

CHAPTER ONE
1959

The 1959 El Caminos were introduced on October 16, 1958, and shared bodies with two other Chevrolets: the Brookwood station wagon which had only one door on each side and the sedan delivery. Two series were offered. The 1180 came with a six-cylinder 135-hp, 235.5-ci engine; and the 1280 came with a 185-hp, 283-ci V-8 engine. Tire size was 8.00x14, although 8.50x14's were optional. Transmission options for the six-cylinder were Powerglide and overdrive. These were also options for the eight-cylinder, which had as additional choices the four-speed synchromesh and Turboglide.

The 1280 had several more powerful engine options, all based on the 348-ci V-8. They all had dual exhausts and included:

250-hp Turbo-Thrust with four-barrel carburetor

280-hp Super Turbo-Thrust with three, two-barrel carburetors

305-hp Turbo-Thrust Special with four-barrel carburetor and high-lift camshaft

315-hp Super Turbo-Thrust Special with three, two-barrel carburetors and high-lift camshaft

320-hp Turbo-Thrust Special with four-barrel carburetor and high-lift camshaft

An advertising photo showing the vehicle's long, low lines. *(Chevrolet)*

335-hp Super Turbo-Thrust Special with three, two-barrel carburetors, high-lift camshaft and mechanical valve lifters.

The powerplants were the same as for other Chevrolets of that year. The six-cylinder engine had been used on passenger cars since 1950. (Prior to this it had been used on Chevrolet trucks but in 1950 it was added to the passenger line since it was needed for coupling with the then-new Powerglide transmission.) The 283-ci V-8 had been introduced in 1957; and the 348-ci V-8, in 1958.

Optional equipment for the 1959 El Caminos included air conditioning (not available with all engines); De Luxe equipment package (right and left armrests, right sunshade, front fender ornaments, and cigarette lighter); E-Z-Eye glass; radio (either manual or push-button); power steering; heavy-duty rear springs; dual-speed windshield wipers; and windshield washers. There were thirteen single-color choices, and ten two-tone color combinations.

As a truck, the 1959 El Camino had the ability to carry 1,200 pounds. This was while using the 8.50x14 tires. With the 8.00x14 tires, the payload was only about 650 pounds. These capacities may be compared with those of other small, conventional pickups offered by Chevrolet that year, which ranged from 1,300 to 1,600 pounds.

Design of the truck-body portion of the El Camino might be described this way: Cut the roof of the station wagon body just behind the driver's seat down to the bottom of where the windows would be; then cut straight back at the level of the window bottoms, keeping the side and rear styling below the line intact. Then, inside the cavity, insert a rear window and panel behind the seat, and place a rectangular pickup box inside the side and tail panels. Styling of the cab resulted in some room behind the seatbacks, and the spare tire was mounted upright, inside the cab, on the rear wall on the passenger's side.

Placing the rectangular box inside the panels resulted in double-wall construction, which was often mentioned as an advantage since dents received from carrying cargo inside the pickup box would not show on the outside. It also meant the tailgate was so thick that it could be opened no further than a level position, which would be a slight disadvantage for certain loading operations. In 1959 (and 1960) models, the rear license plate was mounted on the tailgate, and

The one-time elegance can still be seen in this 1959 model spotted in Fresno. Note rails along rear, the wraparound windshield and rear window and the rear window overhang.

A publicity shot of the 1959 El Camino. *(Chevrolet)*

A view in the mirror that El Camino enthusiasts envy. *(Sue Glasgow)*

El Camino interior for 1959 was done in high fashion with bright, vinyl seat upholstery and new passenger car instrument panel.

the mounting was hinged so that the license could be vertical while the tailgate was down.

Styling is difficult to describe. In retrospect, 1959 Chevrolets suffered from many styling excesses, most of which were incorporated into the El Camino. The cat's-eye taillights were so wide that the narrow part of each had to be incorporated into the tailgate. The decorative fin above each taillight was retained for the El Camino. While the fins may have made backing up to park easier, they seemed only to emphasize the waste of metal which reduced the possible dimensions of the truck body.

Today, 1959 El Caminos can still occasionally be spotted on the street, reminders of a more opulent era in automotive styling. One present-day owner wrote: "The nicest thing about owning a 1959 El Camino in 1980/81 is the unusual-ness about them. You don't see yourself coming down the street every day, in one."

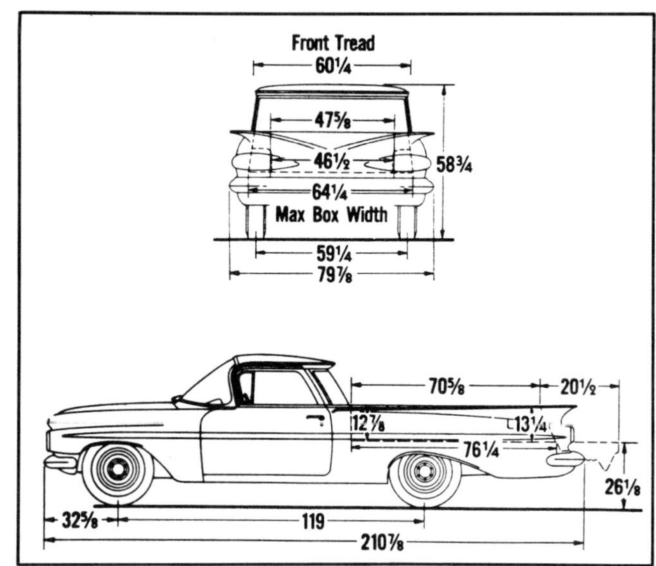

These line drawings for various years are from the truck manuals prepared for dealers. This 1959 model had the most flamboyant styling of all El Caminos. *(Chevrolet)*

View from the rear with tailgate down.

New El Camino presented the crisp, sculptured lines of 1959 Chevrolet passenger car styling, viewed here from the rear.

What's a little more chrome to a '59 Chevy? This El Camino belongs to Jim Slavic and has rally wheels and an additional push bar. *(Jim Slavic)*

This modified 1959 belongs to Morley Brown. This view shows louvered hood, scoop and blower. *(Sue Glasgow)*

CHAPTER TWO
1960

While there were few major changes in the El Camino between the 1959 and 1960 model years, some of the 1959's styling excesses were toned down. The result was possibly the most attractive of all El Caminos. Surprisingly, sales were the lowest for any El Camino model year and, today, 1960 models are rare on the streets. Literature for this model year combined the El Camino and the sedan delivery and was clearly directed at truck buyers.

Two models were again offered. The 1180 came with a six-cylinder engine with ratings similar to those in 1959. The 1280 came with the 283-ci V-8, now rated at 170 hp. Optional V-8 engines were:

230-hp Super Turbo-Fire with 283-ci displacement and a four-barrel carburetor

250-hp Turbo-Thrust with four-barrel carburetor. It and all the engines listed below as 1960 options were based on the 348-ci V-8, and had dual exhausts.

280-hp Super Turbo-Thrust with three, two-barrel carburetors

305-hp Turbo-Thrust Special with four-barrel carburetor and high-lift camshaft

Combining business with pleasure—advertising for 1960 stressed this aspect of El Camino's versatility. *(Chevrolet)*

320-hp Turbo-Thrust Special with four-barrel carburetor and high-lift camshaft

335-hp Super Turbo-Thrust Special with three, two-barrel carburetors, high-lift camshaft and mechanical valve lifters.

Other details concerning equipment, options and capacity show little change from 1959.

Literature for 1960 listed all these engine options, and this was about the only hint that the El Camino might be thought of as a muscle car (or truck, as the case may be). In the 1959 sales literature, only one of the V-8 options had been listed; the others had to be found in the dealers' data book. However, the 1960 literature indicated that the sedan delivery, apparently considered to be more of a truck, had only three engines available—the standard six, the standard V-8, and the 230-hp, 283-ci V-8.

At the end of the 1960 model year, the El Camino line was dropped. This was because the chassis upon which 1959 and 1960 El Caminos were placed was being discontinued, and none of the chassis which was to be used in 1961 was suitable. (This may indicate that the 1959-60 El Caminos were introduced somewhat hurriedly to compete with the Rancheros.) In any event, Chevrolet executives were sufficiently pleased with the El Camino's sales success that they decided to reintroduce it as soon as an acceptable chassis became available. They no doubt noticed that Ford, in 1960, had downsized its Ranchero to the Falcon chassis.

Chevrolet planned to introduce an intermediate-size chassis in 1964 for a model called the Chevelle. This was far enough into the future so that adaptations could be made to accommodate the El Camino's truck-like body. In the meantime, there were to be no El Caminos in the 1961, 1962 or 1963 model lines.

Interior as shown in sales brochure. El Caminos had split seat backs to provide access to rear of cab. Spare tire is visible. *(Chevrolet)*

A 1960 with tonneau cover sitting in Bob Wingate's car lot in San Dimas, California. *(Bob Wingate)*

Randy Aaronian owns this well-preserved 1960 El Camino.

El Camino model 1280 came standard with this tough 170-hp 283-ci Turbo-Fire for 1960. Optional at extra cost for the El Camino were V-8 engines with up to 335 hp.

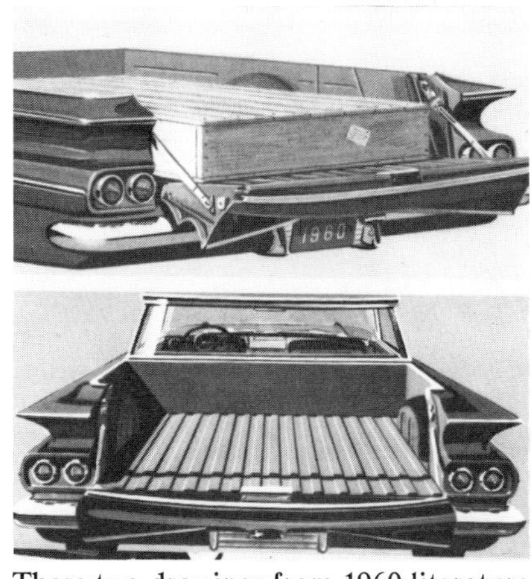

These two drawings from 1960 literature show the tailgates in lowered position. Because of double-walled construction, and the bumper across the entire body, El Camino tailgates could never drop farther. Caption accompanying these 1960 drawings said that when closed, the tailgate provided a "graintight seal," a phrase many truck users would understand. *(Chevrolet)*

The phrase "greenhouse" was often associated with GM autos in 1959 and 1960. It might also apply to this 1960 El Camino.

The 1960 model had plenty of glass around the cab.

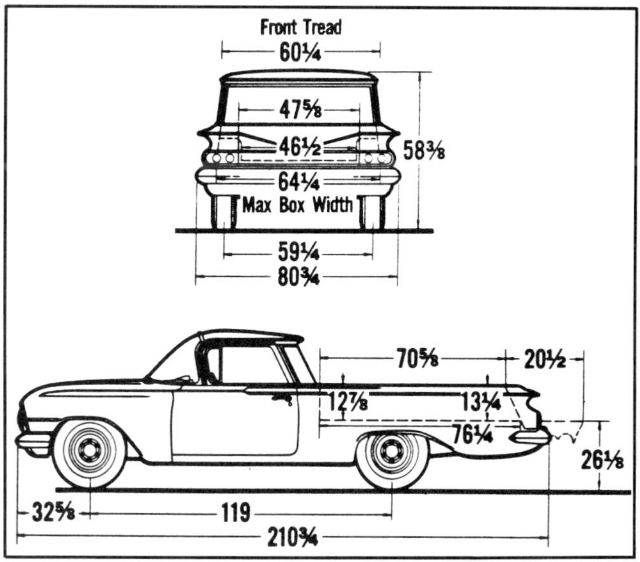

The 1960 model was the same size as the previous year's, but the flared styling in both the front and rear has been toned down. *(Chevrolet)*

A factory photo taken in a nursery setting. *(Chevrolet)*

CHAPTER THREE
1964

The 1964 El Camino was an attractive vehicle based on the Chevelle line. The word Chevrolet appeared above the grille and on the tailgate; Chevelle appeared on both sides just to the rear of the headlights; and El Camino appeared along the sides at the rear.

The truck body had clean lines and none of the unnecessary sheet metal that had graced the 1959 and 1960 models. Approximately the same truck body was to be used through the 1967 models and, from a trucker's perspective, it was to be the most practical of all El Caminos. Despite the fact that it sat on a shorter wheelbase, the truck's pickup box was larger than on the 1959-1960 models, in terms of height and length. It was no wider than on the 1959-60 models, although the tailgate was. The license plate was mounted on the bumper. Payload was rated at 1,200 pounds for the six-cylinder models, and 1,100 pounds for the eight-cylinder models, both on 7.00x14 tires. (Also available were 7.50x14 tires.)

A new feature was air-booster shock absorbers in the rear. Using an air hose from a service station, the owner could increase the air pressure within the rear

"A real dandy . . . plain or fancy" is how El Camino was described in 1964 ads. *(Chevrolet)*

shocks which would allow the El Camino to carry a heavier load. The owner was instructed to keep the shocks at ten-pounds pressure when the vehicle was empty. If planning to carry a heavy load, he was to increase the air pressure to sixty-five pounds, prior to loading. If he loaded first, and then added air, ninety-pounds pressure was required.

Two styles were offered in 1964: the El Camino and the Custom El Camino. On the exterior, the Custom El Camino had additional moldings around the wheel openings, the pickup box, the doors and windshield; and a hood windsplit molding. The standard El Camino's interior was described this way in the dealers' data book: "All-vinyl seat and sidewall trim is featured in the El Camino. Interior components are color-keyed in either fawn, aqua or red. Other interior appointments include: embossed vinyl headlining, dual adjustable sun visors, color-keyed vinyl-coated rubber floor covering, foam-cushioned seats, cigarette lighter, glove compartment lock, adjustable rearview mirror, armrests, center dome light, and bright instrument panel facing, molding and Chevrolet nameplate."

The dealers' data book continued with description of the interior on the Custom El Camino: "In place of the interior appointments described for the El Camino, the Custom El Camino is accented with color-keyed pattern cloth and leather-grain vinyl upholstery, deep-twist carpet floor covering and de luxe door and window regulator handles. Features in addition to those in the El Camino include bright glove compartment door facing and nameplate, glove compartment light, two-tone steering wheel and an electric clock." Bucket seats were available on the Custom El Camino. Fourteen single exterior colors were available, and the accompanying table lists them, along with the interior colors they could be paired with. (The table is from the dealers' data book.) There were no two-tone choices.

Both a six-cylinder and a V-8 were available. The 194-ci six was rated at 120 gross hp, and had been introduced initially in 1962 for the Chevy II. The standard V-8 had 283 cubic inches and was rated at 195 gross hp. Two optional engines were: the 220-hp 283-ci with a four-barrel carburetor and a 250-hp 327-ci version. (All of these engines were available on

The shape and dimensions of the box on the 1964 through 1967 El Caminos. *(Chevrolet)*

Three views of the 1964 model. *(Chevrolet)*

other Chevelles, as well as many other cars in the 1964 Chevrolet model lines.) The 1964 El Camino shared a heavy-duty brake, axle and suspension system with station wagons, a pattern that was to continue for some years.

Some of the options available for the 1964 El Caminos were air conditioning, seat belts, a heavy-duty clutch, a heavy-duty radiator, Posi-traction rear axle, an electric tachometer, power windows and tinted glass. Overdrive and Powerglide options were available for the six; the V-8 could have as options a four-speed floor-shift synchromesh, overdrive or Powerglide.

When analyzing the El Camino's "split personality," one could say that this particular model was closer to the truck image than any other year. Changes which were to take place in the future were not aimed at improving the El Camino's ability to function as a truck.

El Caminos would, from 1964 through 1967, have similar truck bed and cab lines, and a number of camper shell manufacturers began designing shells to fit El Caminos. In a sense, this is surprising since the bodies were low and, from a *camper's* viewpoint, offered little more than covered sleeping space. (Shells offered in later years and pictured elsewhere in this book were often much higher, perhaps reflecting recognition of that shortcoming.) Two West Coast camper shell manufacturers were asked how they designed camper shells to fit El Caminos. Lee C. Stockland, president of the Stockland Company in Irvine, California, replied (in part): "First you have to have a vehicle. The design of the shell is so dependent on the lines of the vehicle that without it we're just stabbing in the dark.

"Second we use cardboard profiles for general outline both from the side and from the rear.

"Third we make a frame that fits the bed rim exactly.

"Fourth we build on the frame the plug, or pattern, out of wood, foam, fiberglass and other material to the shape of the profiles previously cut from the cardboard.

"Fifth we place the plug or pattern back on the vehicle, look at it, change or modify it or in some cases start all over again.

This '64 had side emblems removed and is now a bright yellow with red pinstriping. Old Yeller is painted across tailgate. *(Steve Stefinsky)*

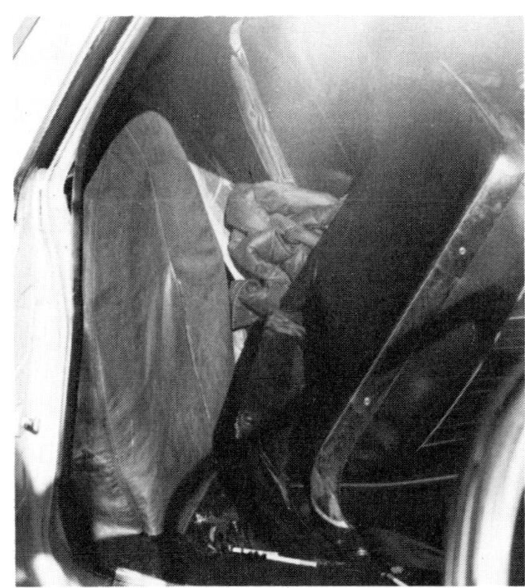

A Fairfax, California, Chevron station uses this 1964 El Camino for service calls. Interior is still in good shape; note spare tire cover. Detail shot shows emblem just in front of taillight.

A 1964 El Camino at Bob Wingate's San Dimas lot. Rear window slides open for access to camper shell. *(Bob Wingate)*

"From this we finish the pattern, make a mold for it, then start producing parts."

Dan Willis, the engineering manager at Gem Top Manufacturing in Clackamas, Oregon, was asked to respond regarding design problems unique to El Camino shells: "The main problem involved in the design of a Gem Top to fit the El Camino is that it must conform to the shape of the vehicle's cab as closely as possible yet leaving room (around the cab) for deviation in manufacturing of the El Camino truck. This is obtained by having a flexible front end on the canopy and a front seal that will take up as much as one-half inch from standard, [this is] unlike other canopies which do not have open front ends and do not seal directly to the top of the truck cab.

"Our second major problem is obtaining a near-perfect roof line, as it is at eye level when installed on the El Camino and any imperfections can be seen very easily. This is obtained by the right combination of ribs, forming of the roof section and thickness of polyurethane spray foam."

Various pictures throughout the book show camper shells, tonneau covers and utility boxes which were available as aftermarket accessories.

EXTERIOR AND INTERIOR COLOR COMBINATIONS

1964 El Camino models have Magic-Mirror Acrylic Lacquer finish for lustrous, long-lasting beauty.

Exterior Color★	Interior Color Availability		
Aqua, Azure ●		Aqua	
Aqua, Lagoon ●		Aqua	
Beige, Desert	Fawn		Red
Black, Tuxedo	Fawn	Aqua	Red
Blue, Daytona ●	Fawn		
Blue, Silver ●	Fawn		
Fawn, Almond ●	Fawn		Red
Green, Bahama ●	Fawn		
Green, Meadow ●	Fawn		
Red, Ember	Fawn		Red
Red, Palomar ●	Fawn		Red
Silver, Satin ●		Aqua	Red
Tan, Saddle ●	Fawn		
White, Ermine	Fawn	Aqua	Red

★El Camino models available with solid exterior colors only.
●Metallic-type paint.

Note flame treatment around front fender. Owner is Roger M. Callies. *(Roger M. Callies)*

This was a publicity photo for Gem Top camper shells. Note how lines of shell matched those of cab. *(Gem Top)*

CHAPTER FOUR
1965

There were relatively few changes from the 1964 models. El Caminos in 1965 continued to have clean, almost Spartan lines and were very attractive in a no-nonsense manner. The word Chevelle was apparently dropped from the El Camino's exterior.

This must be an attractive year for collectors; quite a few '65's were spotted by the author, and many of these had been either well-cared-for or restored. A questionnaire to a sample of El Camino owners asked those who had owned more than one El Camino to indicate which year's model they thought was better or best, and 1965 was frequently mentioned. Dave Moraca, of Paradise Valley, Arizona, said of the 1965 El Camino: "GM made it too good—it won't wear out."

This year, two six-cylinder engines were offered. Standard equipment was the 194-ci with 120 gross hp. The optional six had 230 cubic inches and 140 gross hp. (It had been available on some other Chevrolets, but not the El Camino, in 1964.) Both sixes came with a three-speed transmission, and with either overdrive or Powerglide available at extra cost.

Ads for the 1965 El Camino stressed its luxurious options, rugged build and half-ton-plus cargo capacity. *(Chevrolet)*

The standard 283-ci V-8 engine was rated at 195 hp. The same-size engine was also available with a 220-hp rating. There were three horsepower ratings with the 327-ci engine: 250, 300 and 350. The 250-hp engine had, as an additional option, dual exhausts. The 350 came with a three-speed transmission, or an optional four-speed. Powerglide was available to accompany all other V-8's, and overdrive was available with only the standard V-8.

The 1965 El Caminos rode on larger tires than the 1964 models. New tire size in 1965 was 7.35x14, although 7.75x14's were also available. Payloads for the six-cylinder models now ranged from 1,150 to 1,250 pounds, and from 1,050 to 1,150 pounds for the V-8's.

Two trims were available: standard and custom. The latter was also available with bucket seats. A console was provided when a four-speed transmission was ordered with a V-8 engine.

Note the increase in power options available in this model year. The sales literature emphasized the "personal" small truck. It said: "Personalize the fun-loving El Camino to your heart's content. Power brakes, steering and windows if you wish. Air conditioning, bucket seats and Soft-Ray tinted glass? Of course! Go all the way with a tachometer, Comfortilt 7-position steering wheel . . . with sport-type walnut-grained plastic rim if it suits your fancy. They're all available as extra-cost options for your personal comfort and enjoyment."

This El Camino's owner was restoring its original appearance. Note dual tail pipes.

Neat, uncluttered dash of the 1965 El Camino.

Some additional striping was added to this El Camino.

Dave Moraca owns this 1965 El Camino spotted on the shores of the Great Salt Lake in Utah. Interior shots show bucket seats, and spare tire and fire extinguisher stored behind.

This 1965 model was parked in Fresno.

This 1965 El Camino is unusual from the rear: the left taillight is a standard 1965 edition; while the right one is from a 1964.

1965 emblem for the 283-ci V-8.

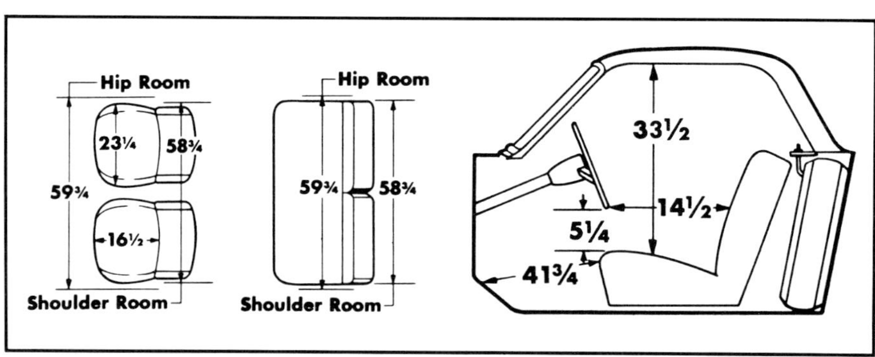

Cab interior dimensions, with two seating options, for 1965 model. Same approximate dimensions held for the 1964 through 1967 El Caminos. *(Chevrolet)*

CHAPTER FIVE
1966

Once again, there were few changes from the previous year's models; but a highlight was the addition of the 396 engine option to the line. The 1966 El Caminos are easy to recognize from behind because their taillights face inward, oblivious to the soon to be mandated requirement that lights be visible from the side.

The same two six-cylinder engines as were offered in 1965 were available in 1966. They came with standard three-speed transmissions, and had Powerglide and 3-speed overdrive options.

The V-8 offerings were changed somewhat. The standard V-8 was still the 283-ci 195-hp version, with an optional 220-hp rating. Four different transmissions complemented them: A three-speed, a four-speed wide-range, Powerglide and 3-speed overdrive. The next larger V-8, available as an option, was the 327-ci, rated at 275 hp, and coming with a three-speed, a four-speed, or a Powerglide transmission. Also offered was the 396-ci with either a 325-hp or a 360-hp rating. The 396 had been introduced by Chevrolet in early 1965, and was to become one of its best-

A '66 El Camino with some of its bigger brothers. *(Chevrolet)*

known high-performance engines in the last half of the 1960's.

With the 1966 El Camino, the 396 325-hp could have a Warner heavy-duty fully synchronized three-speed, a four-speed wide-range or Powerglide. The 360 was available with any of those three, or a four-speed close-ratio. Many of the transmission options available with the V-8's also offered various other powerful rear axle ratios. Tire size was 7.35x14 or 7.75x14, the latter being supplied with the 396-ci engines.

Despite the powerful engines, and accompanying transmissions and axles, available in this—and in subsequent—years, the El Camino never developed much of a reputation as a conventional, stock racer. Its weight distribution was poor, and it fit into no particular race car category. (Some were used for drag racing on streets, or for "off-road" races.) Nonetheless, El Caminos were frequently used by racers to pull trailered race cars, or to carry racing motorcycles in the pickup box.

Trim on the 1966 El Caminos differed little from that offered in previous years. There were standard and custom interior trims, with bucket seats available with the latter. The bucket-seat option came with the choice of fawn, red or black upholstery and interior panels. Interior colors with the conventional seats were fawn, blue or red.

Fifteen exterior colors were available, with no two-tone combinations. Ten of the colors were metallic: mist blue, Danube blue, marina blue, willow green, artesian turquoise, tropic turquoise, Aztec bronze, Madeira maroon, sandalwood tan and chateau slate. The five other colors were tuxedo black, ermine white, regal red, cameo beige and lemonwood yellow.

Sales literature made reference to "Chevelle styling," and front nameplate on some models had Chevelle lettering, while others had El Camino lettering.

For 1966 the custom interior featured richer, all-vinyl upholstery, enhanced by a restyled seat and side panels and a redesigned instrument panel.

Four-season air conditioning kept inside air cool, free of dust and pollen. Heavy-duty radiator, Delcotron generator and fan were included.

New wheel discs were redesigned for 1966 to complement El Camino's new styling. Simulated wire wheel covers were also available, as were whitewall tires.

The owner of this El Camino rigged a clothesline for drying swimsuits. Picture was taken in California's Russian River resort area.

Note high seat backs on this 1966 El Camino. Picture taken in parking lot at a *Truckin'* magazine-sponsored meet for '50's Chevrolet and GMC trucks held in Ogden, Utah, in 1981.

A Chevrolet aficionado. *(Roger M. Callies)*

This well-preserved 1966 El Camino is from the neighborhood where I live. Wording on front emblem is "Chevelle" while tailgate has Chevrolet emblem. Wording on side says "El Camino."

Three views of the 1966 El Camino. *(Chevrolet)*

CHAPTER SIX 1967

This was the last of the El Caminos to be built on the lines introduced in 1964. There were virtually no changes from the previous year's model. Taillights had three-piece lenses and wrapped around the sides of the rear fenders. Between them (across the tailgate) was a vinyl, wood-grain strip. This was the first year that optional vinyl roof tops were offered; they came in either black or beige. Also available as first-time options were front disc brakes, air-pollution control devices (required by the State of California) and head restraints. Another factory option was special wheel covers, with a choice between mag-style and simulated wire. Tire size was 7.35x14, with 7.75x14's coming with the 396 engine.

The major sales brochure had as its theme "The El Camino at work and at play." Under the "at work" heading, reference was made to "a choice of seven spirited engines . . . plus six different transmissions . . . ."; which would seem to be of more interest to muscle car buyers than to truck users. The accompanying table, from a dealers' data book, illustrates the great number of power-team alternatives available to 1967 El Camino buyers. (The 250-ci six, avail-

A 1967 El Camino with a Gem Top camper shell. *(Gem Top)*

able for the first time on El Caminos, had been used on other Chevrolets previously.)

EL CAMINO POWER TEAMS

Engine, Transmission and Rear Axle Combinations

ENGINES: Option	ENGINES: Description	TRANSMISSION	REAR AXLE RATIOS★ Without Air Conditioning: Std	Without Air Conditioning: Optional Econ	Without Air Conditioning: Optional Perf	Without Air Conditioning: Optional Spec	With Air Conditioning: Std	With Air Conditioning: Optional Econ	With Air Conditioning: Optional Perf	With Air Conditioning: Optional Spec
Std on Models 133-13580	**140-hp Turbo-Thrift 230 6-Cylinder** 230-cu-in displacement Single-barrel carburetor 8.5:1 compression ratio Hydraulic valve lifters	Std 3-Speed Full-Synchro Special 3-Speed Full-Synchro Powerglide	3.36:1	3.08:1	3.55:1	3.70:1	3.36:1	—	3.55:1	3.70:1
		Overdrive	3.70:1	—	—	—	3.70:1	—	—	—
L22 on Models 133-13580	**155-hp Turbo-Thrift 250 6-Cylinder** 250-cu-in displacement Single-barrel carburetor 8.5:1 compression ratio Hydraulic valve lifters	Std 3-Speed Full-Synchro Special 3-Speed Full-Synchro	3.08:1	—	3.36:1	3.55:1 or 3.70:1	3.36:1	—	3.55:1	3.70:1
		Powerglide	3.36:1	3.08:1	3.55:1	3.70:1	3.36:1	—	3.55:1	3.70:1
		Overdrive	3.70:1	—	—	—	3.70:1	—	—	—
Std on Models 134-13680	**195-hp Turbo-Fire 283 8-Cylinder** 283-cu-in displacement 2-barrel carburetor 9.25:1 compression ratio Hydraulic valve lifters	Std 3-Speed Full-Synchro Special 3-Speed Full-Synchro 4-Speed Wide-Range Powerglide	3.08:1	—	3.36:1	3.55:1 or 3.70:1	3.36:1	—	3.55:1	3.70:1
		Overdrive	3.70:1	—	—	—	3.70:1	—	—	—
L30 on Models 134-13680	**275-hp Turbo-Jet 327 8-Cylinder** 327-cu-in displacement Regular camshaft 4-barrel carburetor 10.0:1 compression ratio Hydraulic valve lifters	Std 3-Speed Full-Synchro Special 3-Speed Full-Synchro Powerglide	3.08:1	—	3.36:1	3.55:1 or 3.70:1	3.36:1	—	3.55:1	3.70:1
		4-Speed Wide-Range	3.07:1	—	3.31:1	3.55:1 or 3.73:1	3.31:1	—	3.55:1	3.73:1
L79 on Models 134-13680	**325-hp Turbo-Fire 327 8-Cylinder** 327-cu-in displacement High-lift camshaft 4-barrel carburetor 11.0:1 compression ratio Hydraulic valve lifters	Special 3-Speed Full-Synchro 4-Speed Wide-Range	3.31:1	3.07:1	3.55:1	3.73:1	3.31:1	—	3.55:1	3.73:1
		4-Speed Close-Ratio	3.31:1	3.07:1	3.55:1	3.73:1 4.10:1 4.56:1 4.88:1	3.31:1	—	3.55:1	3.73:1
L35 on Models 134-13680	**325-hp Turbo-Jet 396 8-Cylinder** 396-cu-in displacement Regular camshaft 4-barrel carburetor 10.25:1 compression ratio Hydraulic valve lifters Dual exhaust	Special 3-Speed Full-Synchro 4-Speed Wide-Range	3.31:1	3.07:1	3.55:1	3.73:1 or 4.10:1	3.07:1	—	—	—
		Powerglide	3.07:1	2.73:1	3.31:1	3.55:1 3.73:1 4.10:1	3.07:1	—	—	—
		Turbo Hydra-Matic	#2.73:1	—	3.07:1	3.31:1	3.07:1	—	—	—
L34 on Models 134-13680	**350-hp Turbo-Jet 396 8-Cylinder** 396-cu-in displacement High-lift camshaft 4-barrel carburetor 10.25:1 compression ratio Hydraulic valve lifters	Special 3-Speed Full-Synchro 4-Speed Wide-Range	3.55:1	3.31:1	3.73:1	4.10:1	3.07:1	—	—	—
		Powerglide	3.31:1	3.07:1	3.55:1	3.73:1 or 4.10:1	3.07:1	—	—	—
		4-Speed Close-Ratio	3.55:1	3.31:1	3.73:1	3.07:1 4.10:1 4.56:1 4.88:1	3.07:1	—	—	—
		Turbo Hydra-Matic	3.07:1	2.73:1	3.31:1	—	3.07:1	—	—	—

★ All ratios available as positraction. *(4.10:1, 4.56:1 and 4.88:1 available as positraction only.)* See ordering information on page 5.
When G.M. Air Injection Reactor (RPOK19) is ordered with Turbo Hydra-Matic trans. (RPO M40), standard axle is 2.56:1, Performance axle is 2.73:1.

February 1, 1967

Standard interior is shown at top; custom interior at the bottom, in this 1967 sales brochure. *(Chevrolet)*

Note fancy wheel covers on this model for PR photo taken in Detroit. *(Chevrolet)*

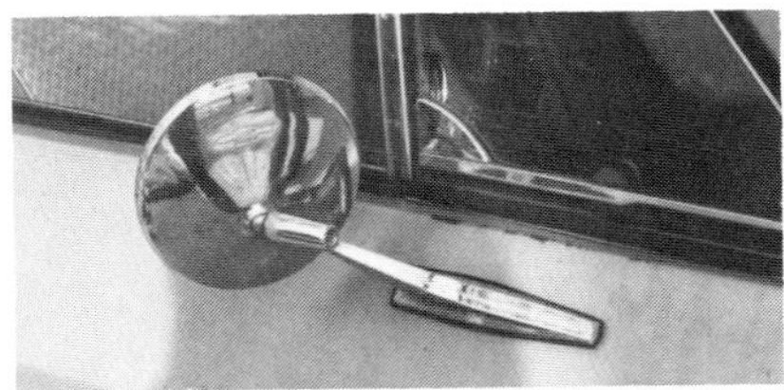

Right-side mirror for the '67. Note the bow-tie emblem near the top.

This 1967 model has a 327-ci engine and a vinyl top.

Front fender line of a '67. Note the El Camino lettering—which changed almost yearly—and the fender emblem for the six-cylinder 250 engine.

Full wheel cover and hub cap for the 1967 El Camino.

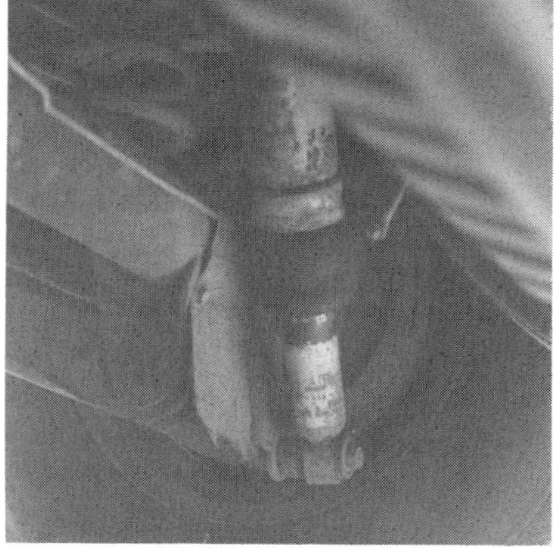

One of the air-adjustable rear shocks.

Close-up of the spare tire location and air filler valve for the rear shocks, located behind the passenger seat.

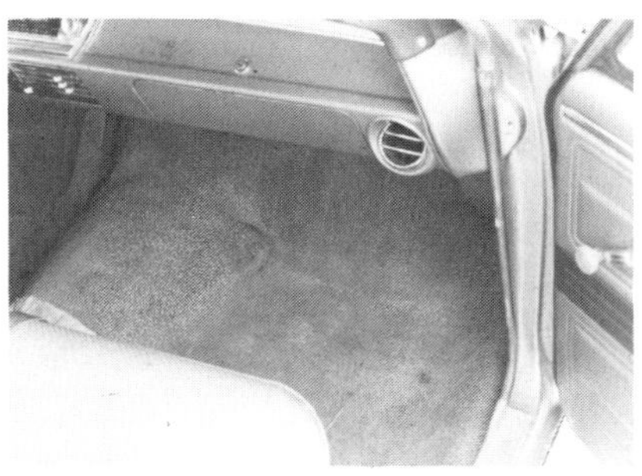

Interior shot of a 1967.

This example was parked in San Rafael, California. The owner said that the vinyl strip between the taillights had been removed, and the area repainted.

CHAPTER SEVEN
1968

A newly designed El Camino was offered in 1968; the truck bed, rear end and cab styling were to hold through 1972 models. For added style, the roof lines sloped downward more gently than the actual slope of the rear window, giving a more streamlined appearance from the side than had been the case with the 1964-67 El Caminos. The pickup box dimensions were virtually the same as for the 1964-67 models. However, overall vehicle length increased, from approximately 197 inches for the 1964-67 El Caminos to 207 inches for the 1968-72's. Virtually all of this increased length was ahead of the pickup box.

Factory literature printed in August 1967 and some ads showed a small, postage-stamp-size, rear-marker light just in front of the top of the rear bumper. However, a page from the dealers' data book printed in February 1968 mentioned front side-marker lights, but not those at the rear. I saw no 1968 El Caminos with rear side-marker lights, although one picture from a 1968 owner showed these lights.

A new line of El Caminos was added this year: the SS, or Super Sport, with special trim, including the SS emblem on the front grille. Also available was special

This 1968 SS 396 was spotted in an Ogden, Utah, used car lot. Rust was just beginning to eat through the finish near the wheel wells. The numbers painted in front of the rear wheel were its estimated maximum weight, for truck registration purposes.

This factory photo of a 1968 SS shows marker lights on the rear. *(Chevrolet)*

A 1968 with 327-ci engine and wide wheels.

This is used by a sheet metal shop. Malibu appears on front fender, designating the "better" line of Chevelles.

SS side striping. The SS came with six-inch-wide rims, while most other El Caminos used five-inch rims. Curb (empty) weights of the various 1968 El Camino models give an idea as to the 396's heavy engine. Curb weight for the standard six-cylinder was 3,206 pounds; for the standard V-8 (307-ci), 3,350 pounds; and for the SS 396, the curb weight was 3,675 pounds! Terry Boyce's book, *Chevy Super Sports 1961-1976* (Osceola, WI: Motorbooks International, 1981), focuses on this high-performance Chevrolet and covers well its relationship with, and incorporation into, the El Camino line. This was, of course, the heyday of power, speed and cheap gasoline.

There were two levels of interior trim for the 1968 El Caminos: standard and custom. Strato-bucket seats were available with the custom interior and a console could be obtained with some transmissions.

The standard 230-ci six-cylinder engine developed 140 gross hp. The optional six had 250 cubic inches and 155 horsepower. Available transmissions were a standard three-speed, a heavy-duty three-speed, overdrive and Powerglide.

The standard V-8 was the new 200-hp Turbo-Fire 307, and it could be coupled with any of the four transmissions listed for the six-cylinder. In addition, it could be paired with a four-speed wide-range. The SS came with the 325-hp Turbo-Jet 396 engine, and could be coupled with a Warner heavy-duty three-speed, a four-speed wide-range, Powerglide or Turbo Hydra-matic. Other V-8 engines available were: 250-hp Turbo-Fire 327; 275-hp Turbo-Fire 327; 325-hp Turbo-Fire 327 with high-lift camshaft and dual exhaust; and 350-hp Turbo-Jet 396 with high-lift camshaft and dual exhaust (available on the SS only).

The SS was, and is, an attractive high-powered vehicle. Its introduction, and success (5,190 units were sold in 1968), indicate that one very obvious market of the El Camino was that of the high performance enthusiast.

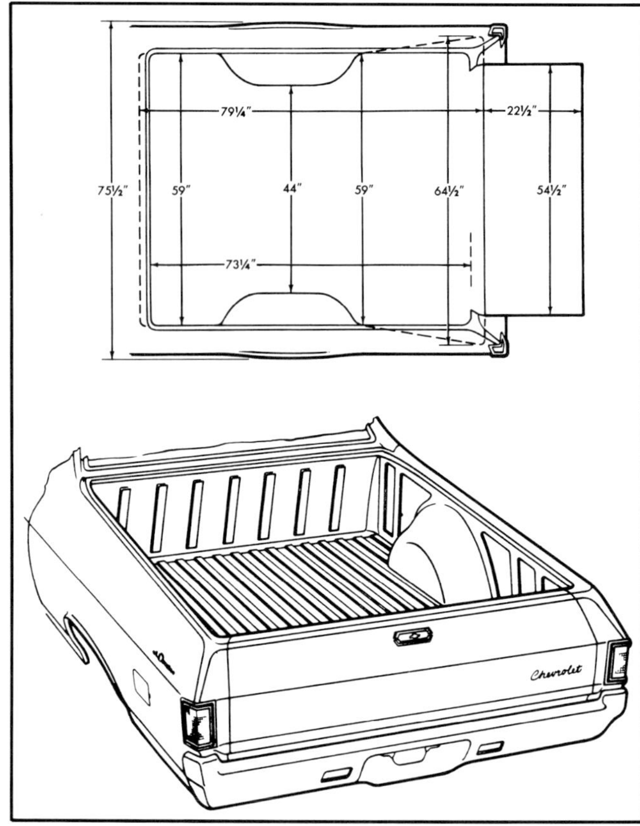

This box was used on the 1968 through 1972 El Caminos. *(Chevrolet)*

This 1968 El Camino was on display at the San Francisco Hot Rod show in late 1981. It has a 327-ci engine. Owner is Mike Menesini.

Referred to as a Camperette, this flat El Camino cover could be opened to provide a tent. When not in use, the canvas would be stored under the closed cover. Manufacturer was Protect-O-Top of Sunnyvale, California. *(Protect-O-Top)*

CHAPTER EIGHT
1969

While the only styling changes for 1969 El Caminos appear to be in the front grille, the result was very attractive. A number of the El Camino owners surveyed picked the 1969 model as being the best looking. Sherman Mehlhoff, of California, said of the '69's: "I like the body style. It's sporty looking."

Will Sibbald, of Louisiana, said: "Without question, one of the nicest designs ever for a car or truck."

Seven engines were offered, including the same two sixes which were offered the previous year. The standard V-8 was the 307-ci with 200 gross hp. One new optional V-8 was the 350-ci, which had been available on other Chevrolet lines earlier, and which came with either a 250-hp or a 300-hp rating. The 396-ci was available only with the SS option, and had a choice of 325, 350 or 375 hp. Numerous transmissions were offered including both a standard and a special three-speed; a four-speed wide-range, a four-speed close-ratio and a four-speed heavy-duty close-ratio; Powerglide; overdrive; and Turbo Hydra-matic. (Some transmissions could not be linked with certain engines.) V-8's were a popular choice for powering El Caminos at this time. George H. Dammann, in his

Rear view of a 1969 SS which was used in El Camino literature. *(Chevrolet)*

Sixty Years of Chevrolet, noted that ninety-four percent of the 1969 El Caminos sold were equipped with V-8 engines. Buyers of sporty, high-performance vehicles often want a range of tires from which to choose. The accompanying table, from the 1969 dealers' data book, indicates all of the *optional* tires one might have installed at the factory.

This year's SS was considered a V-8 model option, rather than a separate model, as had been the case in 1968. Here's the SS description from the dealers' data book: "SS 396: Custom El Camino model only. Includes 325-hp Turbo-Jet 396 engine with bright accents; power front disc brakes; floor-mounted special 3-speed transmission; dual exhausts; black-painted grille; special hood, ornamentation and suspension; wheel opening moldings; 14" x 7" sport wheels and G70-14 special red stripe tires."

The book went on to describe the other engines available: the 350-hp and the 375-hp (which was also available with aluminum cylinder heads). Two special colors were available only with the SS option: Monaco orange and Daytona yellow.

Both standard and custom interiors were offered, and Strato-bucket seats were available with the latter and also with the SS option. Only solid exterior colors were offered although a vinyl roof cover was available in five colors: black, dark blue, parchment, dark brown and midnight green.

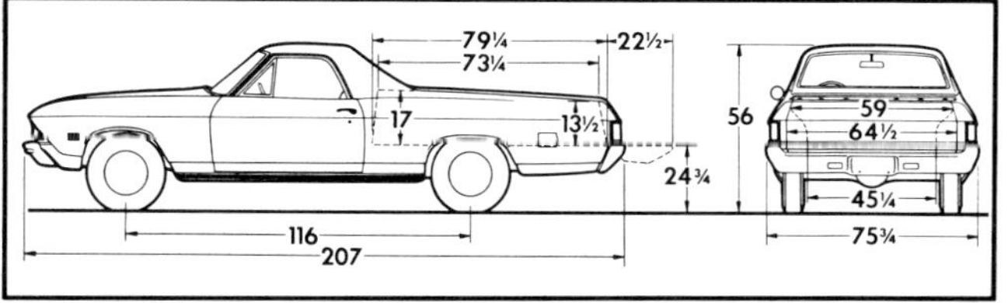

These views are of the 1968 El Camino, and show the shape of the new cab. Vehicle has less of a "boxy" shape than the models for 1964-67. The general lines shown here for the 1968 models continued through the 1972 models. *(Chevrolet)*

An SS 396 which came with a black grille and a special domed hood. Mural on tailgate shows an El Camino (above license plate).

This attractive camper shell even has a luggage rack on top.

A camper shell manufactured by the Stockland Company in Southern California. Starting with 1968 models, the sides of the El Camino's box sloped downward to the rear, and camper shells had to compensate for this by being higher at the rear. *(The Stockland Company)*

Cover photo on 1969 literature. *(Harrah's Automobile Collection)*

CHAPTER NINE
1970

This year's El Camino had attractive lines. For the first time in several years, only one six-cylinder engine was available: a 250-ci rated at 155 gross hp. The standard V-8 was the 307 rated at 200 gross. Wheel size continued to be 14x5 with the standard tire being the F78-14B.

The year 1970 was, according to Terry Boyce's *Chevy Super Sports 1961-1976,* when GM's top management lifted the ban on engines larger than 400 cubic inches for intermediate Chevrolets. El Camino literature for 1970 models, issued in August 1969, indicated that a 400-ci V-8 was available (and it was the 396 with a slightly larger bore). Boyce says that the engine had 402 cubic inches, and he believes that—after January 1, 1970—this was the true size of the engine produced even though many continued to be marketed as "396's" since that designation was so well-known. A larger engine became available for the 1970 El Caminos: the 454. A page from the dealers' data book, issued on January 30, 1970, is reproduced here listing all the available engines, including the 454 with its two horsepower ratings. A comparison between this sheet and the one which ap-

A well-preserved 350.

A 1970 SS which was for sale by Bob Wingate's Classics in Southern California. *(Bob Wingate)*

peared earlier for 1967 El Caminos, shows how their available power packages had increased in engine size. The 1970 El Camino with a 454 must have performed like the proverbial "Bat out of Hell!"

To this point, no mention has been made of prices. Price changes are difficult to trace over the years because features that are standard in some years are optional in others. Also, inflation takes its toll. Nonetheless, for readers who like to recall what a dollar—or, in this case, several thousand dollars—used to buy, here are Chevrolet Division's suggested 1970 retail prices (exclusive of destination charges):

6-cylinder with standard interior $2,677
6-cylinder with custom interior $2,758
Standard V-8 with standard interior $2,769
Standard V-8 with custom interior $2,850

The SS option with the 350-hp Turbo-Jet 396 engine cost an additional $455; and with the 360-hp Turbo-Jet 454 engine, $514. For an additional $269, *plus* the $514, one could have the 454 Turbo-Jet with a 450-hp rating. The SS came with 14x7 sport wheels.

Other V-8 engine options and their costs were as follows: 250-hp Turbo-Fire 350 (for regular-grade fuel), $22; 300-hp Turbo-Fire 350, $70; and 330-hp Turbo-Jet 400, $166. Transmissions and their costs coupled to a V-8 were: Powerglide, $178; Turbo Hydra-matic, $205 to $297, depending upon engine; four-speed wide-range, $189; four-speed close-ratio, $189; and special four-speed close-ratio, $227. A Positraction rear axle cost $43. Power brakes cost either $43 or $66, depending upon whether the El Camino came with disc or drum-type front brakes. Power steering cost between $102 and $108, depending upon the model in which it would be used.

Some other options and their prices follow:

Air conditioning $384
Console, for shift lever $55
Emission control package (required for California) $38
Exhausts, dual $31
Glass, Soft-Ray $37
Hood with "cowl induction" (for SS) $124
Instrumentation (clock, tachometer, ammeter, etc.) $86
Moldings, for windows $22
Radiator, heavy-duty $15

Two views of a 1970 model with a 350-ci engine.

Owner Tony Kemp, of Indiana, sits with his legs inside the open sunroof of his "Black Knight." Note smoked glass in cab. The wide stripe on sides, front and rear is blue and purple. Car is equipped with stock 350 engine, half-moon chrome plates on headlight tops, and has pinstriping on air dam. *(Tony Kemp)*

This El Camino, parked in downtown Sonoma, has extra-wide tires.

Radio, AM $62
Radio, AM-FM $137
Roof cover, vinyl $65
Seats, Strato-bucket $124
Speed and cruise control $59
Steering wheel, Comfortilt $46
Stripe package (for SS) $43
Wheels, rally $37

In addition to listed options and accessories, it was possible—through use of an enterprising dealer—to acquire and have installed equipment intended for other Chevrolet and GM lines. There was—and is—also interchangeability between models of various years.

One last comment to be made about 1970 El Caminos is that they are especially popular for "customizing." In the course of preparing this book, I came across many more owners of customized 1970 models than held true for any other model year.

ENGINES		TRANSMISSIONS	SHIFT LEVER LOCATION		REAR AXLE RATIOS★		
Option Number and Model Application	Description	Type (Std or Optional)	Without Console	With Optional Console	Std	Optional	
						Perf	Trailering
STANDARD ENGINES							
Standard Six-Cylinder on El Camino 6-Cyl Models	**155-hp Turbo-Thrift 250 6-Cylinder** 250-cu-in displacement Single barrel carburetor 8.5:1 compression ratio Hydraulic valve lifters Single exhaust	**3-Speed—Std**	Column	Not Available	3.36	—	—
		Powerglide—M35	Column	In Console w/Floor Shift	3.36	—	—
		Turbo Hydra-matic—M40	Column	In Console w/Floor Shift	3.08	—	—
Standard Eight-Cylinder on El Camino V8 Models	**200-hp Turbo-Fire 307 8-Cylinder** 307-cu-in displacement Regular camshaft 2-barrel carburetor 9.00:1 compression ratio Hydraulic valve lifters Single exhaust	**3-Speed—Std**	Column	Not Available	3.36	—	—
		Powerglide—M35	Column	In Console w/Floor Shift	3.36	—	—
		Turbo Hydra-matic—M40 Without Special Suspension	Column	In Console w/Floor Shift	3.08	—	—
		With Special Suspension	Column	In Console w/Floor Shift	3.08	—	3.31
		4-Speed Wide-Range—M20	Floor With Boot	In Console	3.36	—	—
OPTIONAL ENGINES							
L65 on El Camino V8 Models	**250-hp Turbo-Fire 350 8-Cylinder** 350-cu-in displacement Regular camshaft 2-barrel carburetor 9.00:1 compression ratio Hydraulic valve lifters Single exhaust	**3-Speed—Std**	Column	Not Available	3.08	—	—
		Powerglide—M35	Column	In Console w/Floor Shift	2.73	—	—
		Turbo Hydra-matic—M40 Without Special Suspension	Column	In Console w/Floor Shift	2.56	—	—
		With Special Suspension	Column	In Console w/Floor Shift	2.56	—	3.31
		4-Speed Wide-Range—M20	Floor With Boot	In Console	3.36	—	—
L48 on El Camino V8 Models	**300-hp Turbo-Fire 350 8-Cylinder** 350-cu-in displacement Regular camshaft 4-barrel carburetor 10.25:1 compression ratio Hydraulic valve lifters Single exhaust	**Powerglide—M35**	Column	In Console w/Floor Shift	2.73	—	—
		Turbo Hydra-matic—M40 Without Special Suspension	Column	In Console w/Floor Shift	2.73	—	—
		With Special Suspension	Column	In Console w/Floor Shift	2.73	—	3.31
		4-Speed Wide-Range—M20	Floor With Boot	In Console	3.31	—	—
LS3 on El Camino V8 Models	**330-hp Turbo-Jet 400 8-Cylinder** 400-cu-in displacement Regular camshaft 4-barrel carburetor 10.25:1 compression ratio Hydraulic valve lifters Dual exhausts	**Turbo Hydra-matic—M40** Without Special Suspension	Column	In Console w/Floor Shift	2.73	—	—
		With Special Suspension	Column	In Console w/Floor Shift	2.73	—	3.31
		4-Speed Wide-Range—M20	Floor With Boot	In Console	3.31	—	—
SS 396 Option Z25 on V8 Custom El Camino Model	**350-hp Turbo-Jet 396 8-Cylinder** 396-cu-in displacement High-lift camshaft 4-barrel carburetor 10.25:1 compression ratio Hydraulic valve lifters Dual exhausts	**Turbo Hydra-matic—M40**	Column	In Console w/Floor Shift	3.31	—	—
		4-Speed Wide-Range—M20	Floor With Boot	In Console	3.31	—	—
		4-Speed Close-Ratio—M21	Floor With Boot	In Console	3.31	—	—
SS 454 Option Z15 on V8 Custom El Camino Model	**360-hp Turbo-Jet 454 8-Cylinder** 454-cu-in displacement High-lift camshaft 4-barrel carburetor 10.25:1 compression ratio Hydraulic valve lifters Dual exhausts	**Turbo Hydra-matic—M40**	Column	In Console w/Floor Shift	3.31	—	—
		Special 4-Speed Close-Ratio—M22	Floor With Boot	In Console	3.31	—	—
SS 454 Option Z15/LS6 on V8 Custom El Camino Model	**450-hp Turbo-Jet 454 8-Cylinder** 454-cu-in displacement Special camshaft 4-barrel carburetor 11.25:1 compression ratio Mechanical valve lifters Dual exhausts	**Turbo Hydra-matic—M40**	Column	In Console w/Floor Shift	3.31	4.10	—
		Special 4-Speed Close- Ratio—M22	Floor With Boot	In Console	3.31	4.10	—

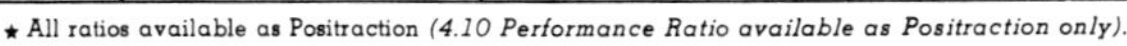

★ All ratios available as Positraction *(4.10 Performance Ratio available as Positraction only).*

Tomm Davis, of Indiana, has extensively customized this 1970 350. The four gauges are on the back of the scoop and are read through the windshield. *(Tomm Davis)*

CHAPTER TEN 1971

In styling, the most obvious change for 1971 was that El Caminos had only one pair of single headlights in front. The rest of the body showed little change from the previous year, or, actually since the 1968 models.

Another significant change was the introduction of a first cousin to the El Camino, known as the GMC Sprint. GMC truck dealers had wanted a GMC truck version of the El Camino for two reasons. First, many of them wanted one for use as one of their own dealership's light delivery trucks. Second, many (actually, most) GMC truck dealers also sold several other GM lines of automobiles such as Pontiacs or Oldsmobiles and since, by now, the El Camino was an established muscle car, they wanted a chance to sell some. (The alternative would have been to produce El Caminos with names of other GM auto lines, but this would have been awkward since they did not produce "trucks" and—as the introductory chapter pointed out—the partial fiction of being a truck was still important.) The GMC version of the El Camino continues to this day although, in 1978, it became known as the Caballero. It accounts for about ten percent of El Camino's sales volume. (See Appendix.)

According to the literature, added years of useful life resulted from a generous application of zinc chromate rust primer to all exposed parts of the 1971 Sprint. And smooth, one-piece fender liners protected fender underbody against flying objects, mud and water.

Within the corporate hierarchy of General Motors, Chevrolet Division designs the smaller trucks, which are then marketed with either Chevrolet or GMC truck nameplates by Chevrolet or GMC truck dealers, respectively. Larger trucks are designed by the staff of GMC Truck and Coach Division and, again, have either Chevrolet or GMC truck nameplates attached and are sold by the respective dealers. Within this arrangement, GMC truck people have very little to say about El Camino designs.

The only differences between El Caminos and the GMC Sprint/Caballeros are the nameplates and, for a few years, some minor cosmetic trim. Despite this, the GMC truck reputation for quality lives on. One of the individuals contacted in the survey, wrote: "I own a GMC Sprint which is not an El Camino. I feel that the Sprint was a better quality auto than the El Camino."

The standard El Camino six had a 250-ci engine with a gross horsepower rating of 145. The standard V-8 was the 307 with 200 hp. There were several optional V-8 engines: the 350 rated at either 245 or 270 hp; the 300-hp Turbo-Jet 400; and—available on the SS only—the Turbo-Jet 454 rated at either 365 or 425 hp. There was a choice of six transmissions, although some could not be coupled with specific engines.

This year, the six-cylinder came with the standard trim only. V-8's could have either standard or custom trim; and those equipped with either the 400- or the 454-ci engine could have the SS trim option as well. Standard wheel size remained the same and the standard tire was E78-14B. The SS came with 15x7 wheels.

The GMC Sprint was available with standard and custom trim only. It had the same seven engines as the El Camino. The Sprint sales brochure made reference to "eight transmissions" but said nothing else about them. (The El Camino brochure had listed six.)

Discussion of El Caminos of this era has concentrated on their increased engine size and said little about their functions as a truck. The two are not unrelated since El Caminos (and Sprints) were often used for pulling trailers, where the extra power often would come in handy. Dealers' data book usually pointed out the special axle and suspension options which were recommended for trailering.

The foam-cushioned, full-bench vinyl seat was available in many colors for the 1971 Sprint. Door and sidewall panels were finished in matching vinyl. The custom interior shown features color-keyed carpeting and vinyl wood-grain trim.

Ayr-Way used this 1971 El Camino for publicity shots of its camper shells. *(Ayr-Way Industries, Inc.)*

The rack was built for carrying pipes, and the close-up picture shows how the racks can be removed from the holders. A thumbscrew holds them tight.

An El Camino 350.

A camper shell made by the Stockland Company is shown on this El Camino 350. Note wide trim strip at bottom of vehicle's body. *(The Stockland Company)*

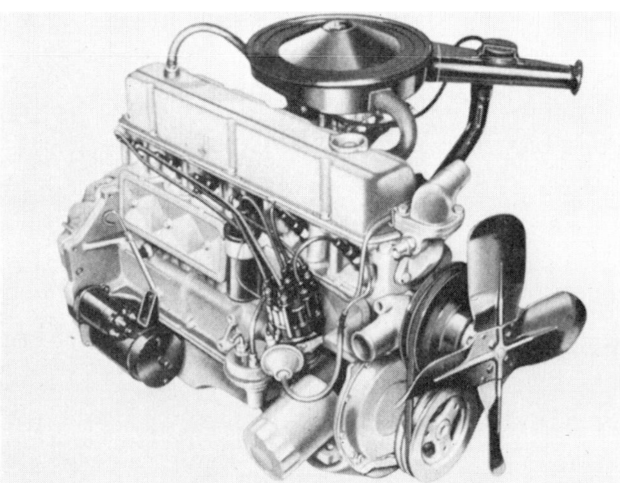

The GMC Sprint's 250 six.

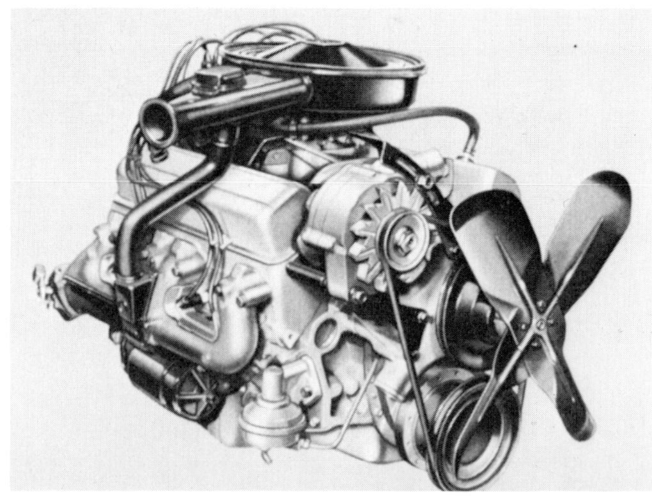

The GMC Invader V-8 for 1971 ran on the new no-lead/low-lead or regular gasoline. Some features included precision-cast cylinder block and heads, independently mounted valve rocker design and positive crankcase ventilation.

CHAPTER ELEVEN
1972

El Caminos and Sprints for 1972 showed little change over the previous year's models. There was little apparent need to tamper with a successful formula; combined sales for both makes increased forty percent over sales of 1971 models! The El Camino was still considered to be part of the Chevelle line, and this would be the last year for the El Camino pickup box and rear end which had been introduced in 1968.

Six out of the ten engines available on Chevrolets this year could be placed in an El Camino. The six-cylinder El Camino came with standard trim only. Its 250-ci engine was now rated at 110 *net* hp (actually the same as the engine offered in 1970 and 1971). It came with a three-speed transmission or with the optional Powerglide.

The V-8 was available with either standard or custom trim and the standard 307-ci engine was rated at 130 net hp. Optional V-8's and their ratings in net horsepower were: 350-ci, with either 165 or 175 hp; the 400 with 240 hp; and the 454 with 270 hp (available on the SS only). The 175-hp and the 240-hp could also be purchased for the SS. Transmissions accompanying the V-8's were the standard three-speed with

A 1972 with 350-ci engine and lower side moldings.

column shift, a special three-speed with floor shift, Powerglide, Turbo Hydra-matic, a four-speed wide-range, a special four-speed close-ratio and one other special three-speed for use with only the 240-hp Turbo-Jet 400 engine.

The dealers' data book gave this description for the SS option: "SS Equipment: Custom El Camino model with optional engine and transmission only. Includes power disc/drum brakes; black-finished grille; special domed hood with locking pins; left-hand remote-control mirrors; SS emblems on fenders and tailgate; 15" x 7" wheels with bright lug nuts, special center caps and trim rings plus F60-15 white lettered tires."

Fifteen solid exterior colors were offered, along with five color choices for vinyl tops: black, light covert, medium green, medium tan and white. In mid-model year, two additional vinyl top colors became available: medium blue and silver pewter.

The GMC Sprint was available with the same engines; although the 240-net-hp version was listed as having *402* cubic inches. The various V-8 engines were referred to by the "Invader" prefix or name. The new Sprint model was the "SP" similar to the El Camino SS, available with SP emblems, dull-black grille, domed hood, etc. In only a year, the Sprint's literature had been recast into a "muscle" vehicle theme, saying, for the 1972 model: ". . . Sprint is a practical business vehicle," but, continuing, ". . . from an appearance standpoint, Sprint says some very special things about its owner. Even more, Sprint has some very special virtues. For personal use, it can be equipped with GMC's Invader 454 CID V-8, close-ratio, four-on-the-floor, proper rear end ratio and SP Equipment. All that, teamed with the ability to do an honest day's labor."

Several of the El Camino and Sprint V-8 engines offered in 1972 were not eligible for vehicle registration in California, because of that state's controls on automotive emissions.

A 1972 El Camino being used by a flea market vender. Stripe along bottom is of "silver" paint and was included with the Custom models that year. View from front shows a Mack Bulldog hood ornament.

A GMC Sprint, a version of the El Camino, was marketed by GMC truck dealers. The model shown had a domed hood and hood hold-down pins. *(National Automotive History Collection, Detroit Public Library)*

Chevrolet dealers were supplied with "flame" decals to install on El Caminos. Decal kits cost approximately $65 and took four hours to install. *(Chevrolet)*

Rear view of a 1972 model showing the vinyl wood-grain strip, backup lights and reflectors on either side of the license.

A Custom El Camino in the foreground and the standard version in the rear. *(Chevrolet)*

The 1972 SS pictured on the front of this sales brochure has a domed hood and hood locking pins. *(Harrah's Automobile Collection)*

This 1972 was modified extensively. The engine is from a 1974 Olds Cutlass 350 and transmission, transfer case, differentials and drive shafts are from a 1975 Blazer. *(Skip Lecates)*

A 1972 El Camino parked on a steep San Francisco hill.

CHAPTER TWELVE
1973

An entirely new cab and truck box design were offered on this year's El Camino. The design would stay in use through the 1977 models. Sales of 1973 El Caminos and Sprints totaled 71,753 units, an all-time record which has never yet been equaled. (This was the last full model year before the first gas crunch.)

The rear lights were circular, and mounted in the lower bumper, two on each side. Some superfluous metalwork extended downward from the top of the cab, in a gentle flowing line along both sides of the truck bed. Minor curves at the rear of the truck body would be at the expense of available loading dimensions. However, the dimensions of the pickup box were nearly the same as on the previous years' El Caminos. The vehicle's wheelbase remained the same, at 116 inches, although overall length increased by six inches to 213. The El Camino's curb weight also increased: in 1972 a V-8 had weighed 3,438 pounds; in 1973, it weighed 3,725 pounds. Maximum payload was about 1,300 pounds. Reflecting this weight increase, and the fact that no six-cylinder engines were offered this year, was the increase in gasoline-tank capacity from nineteen to twenty-six gallons.

A 1973 with SS emblem on grille. The SS option trim also included side stripes which this vehicle does not have.

The standard engine was a 307-ci V-8 rated at 115 net hp. Optional engines were the 350 with a rating of either 145 or 175 net hp, or the 454 with 245 net hp. The Turbo Hydra-matic transmission was available with all four engines, and the three-speed standard was available with the smaller two. A four-speed wide-range could be purchased with the 175-hp 350; and a four-speed close-ratio could be purchased with the 454. Wheel size was now 14x6 with standard tires being G78-14B. The SS had 14x7 wheels.

Both a standard and a custom El Camino were offered, and the SS option was available with the custom El Camino. A new trim option was also offered with the custom El Camino, called the Estate—it had a wood-grain appearance on its sides and on the tailgate.

The dealers' data book described the equipment on each of the 1973 models. The standard El Camino had these features:

EXTERIOR FEATURES

Bright Appearance Items:

"El Camino" Nameplate: On grille panel, LH side
Chevrolet Emblem: Mounted center of grille
Back window reveal moldings
"El Camino" Nameplate: Mounted lower RH side of tailgate
Chrome front and rear bumpers
Door Lock Handles
Door Lock Cylinder Covers
"El Camino" Nameplate: Side of front fenders
Grille outer edge moldings
Head lamp bezel bead
Hood molding
Hub caps
LH side rearview mirror
Side door belt moldings
Tailgate and pickup box belt moldings
Windshield reveal moldings

Doors: RH and LH side doors and tailgate

Door Opening and Lock Methods: Side doors; lift bar latch release with key lock cylinder
Tailgate; single handle double latch

Glass: Windshield, side door drop glass in each door and back glass

A 1973 SS. Small number on grill is 454, the engine size.

This El Camino owner uses the space behind the seat to store his fly rods. In upper left of photo see the edge of the spare tire, which is carried in the box.

A 1973 with optional side molding.

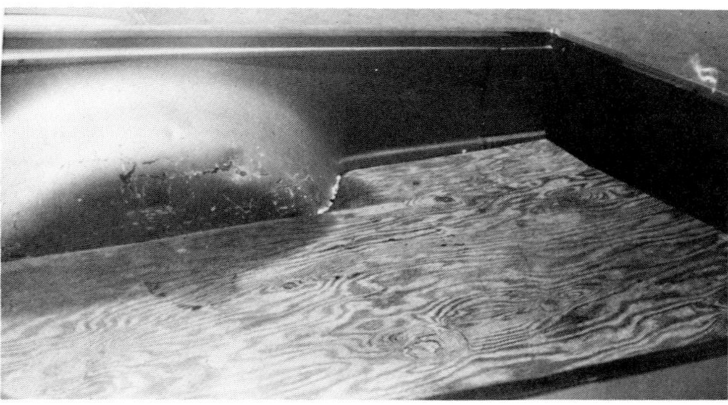

This plywood sheet covered the original floor.

Grille: Plastic grid; painted argent

Instrument Panel Knobs: Marked with function symbols

Lights:

Back-up lights

Combination parking/direction. Two front; single lens

Combination tail/stop/direction/side marker. Two rear Class A

Headlights: Two; Power Beam

License plate: single rear

Side marker and reflectors: 2 front and 2 rear

Mirror: LH chrome fixed arm with 5″ rectangular head

Horn: Single "D" note

Side Door Beams: Steel beam running full width inside each side door

Tools: Mechanical jack; wheel wrench

Undercoating: Partial under body and full under wheel houses

Wheels: Painted body color

Windshield Wipers and Washers: Electric; 2-speed wipers, hideaway wipers and arms

INTERIOR FEATURES

Air Vents: RH and LH cowl side; individually controlled

Arm Rests: RH and LH full depth

Ash Tray

Bright Metal Items:

Control knobs with black accents

Seat back latch and adjuster knobs

Window regulator knobs

Cigarette Lighter

Colors, Interior:

Paint: Same as exterior main color choice

Trim: Black

Courtesy Light Switches: Door actuated dome lamp

Door Lock: Inside; pushbutton lock/release

Door Seals: Closed-cell-type rubber

Floor Mat: Color keyed, vinyl covered rubber

Instruments:

Gauges: Speedometer, odometer and fuel

Switches: Exterior lights, instrument lights, dome light, wiper-washer, headlight beam (foot), ignition, directional signal with lane change position, hazard warning and heater

This 1973 ad shows the location of the valve for adjusting air pressure in rear shocks, at the place where the lower left nut and bolt would be for the rear license plate.

This 1973 GMC Sprint, the High Sierra model, has imitation wood-grain trim along the sides, similar to the trim on the El Camino Estate model.

This custom El Camino, with the Estate trim and a 350 engine, was pictured on the cover of the 1973 literature. *(Harrah's Automobile Collection)*

Warning Lights: Generator, oil pressure, engine temperature, brake warning, direction signals and high beam
Instrument Panel: Fiberglass filled plastic
Heater and Defroster: Deluxe-air
Interior Lights: Instrument and dome operated by main light switch
Insulation and Sound Deadening: Dash (firewall), under floor mat and other strategic points
Mirror, Rearview: Inside 12" wide
Seat: Full width, textured all-vinyl trim
Seat and Shoulder Belts: 3 sets of seat belts; 2 shoulder belts in outboard positions
Steering Wheel: Black grained plastic with soft rim; brushed chrome insert with "Chevrolet" name
Sunshades: RH and LH padded vinyl
Scuff Plate: Side door opening protection and floor mat retainer
Spare Tire Carrier: Inside behind seat on driver side
Steering Lock: Column mounted combination ignition switch, transmission lock, steering lock and accessory switch
Trim Panels: Vinyl door trim panels with bright trim, vinyl coated cowl side panels and vinyl coated headliner
Warning Buzzer: Ignition key removal warning; activated by opening side door with key in switch
Window Regulator Knobs: Bright metal
Windshield Pillar Pads

The custom El Camino had these additional features:

EXTERIOR FEATURES
Bright Appearance Items:
Lower body sill moldings
INTERIOR FEATURES
Carpeting: Color keyed
Colors, Interior Trim: Choice of black or light neutral
Headliner: Deluxe vinyl coated
Instrument Panel Crown Pad and dull paint finish
Mirror; Rearview: Black finish on back and support
Seat: Full-width with custom vinyl trim

The custom El Camino with the SS option had these features in addition to the custom features just listed:

A 1973 model with special striping. Note padlocked trunk in bed.

EXTERIOR FEATURES

Bright Appearance Items:

"SS" emblem on front fender sides, grille and tailgate
Side drip moldings
Wheel opening moldings

Grille: Painted black with center "SS" emblem

Mirrors: Body color racing type; LH remote control, RH manual

Tires: G70-14 Bias belted white lettered

Stripes: Upper body side and tailgate

Turbine I Wheels: 14" x 7"

INTERIOR FEATURES

Seat: Full width with special pattern and custom vinyl trim

"SS" emblem nameplate: On door trim panels and center of steering wheel shroud

Trim Panels, Doors: Special vinyl covered pattern

The custom model with the Estate trim option had these features, plus the other custom features:

EXTERIOR FEATURES

Bright Appearance Items:

Body side and tailgate moldings
"Estate" script nameplate on side of front fenders (below "El Camino" plate)
Wheel opening moldings

Woodgrain Panel: Body sides and tailgate, below moldings

Once again El Caminos were available with two-tone paint (actually only a white top with six different bottom choices). The accompanying chart, from the dealers' data book, shows the varying paint, vinyl roof and interior colors available for 1973.

Despite the fact we're dealing with a muscle car, the sales literature this year made numerous references to the El Camino's being a truck. Across the brochure's cover were the words "1973 Chevrolet Trucks," and in considerably smaller type, "El Camino." On one of the interior pages were a paragraph and bar chart indicating that Chevrolet trucks last longer, and figures were given for the percent of 1957 to 1969 Chevrolet trucks still in use in 1972.

Sprints this year were essentially the same as El Caminos. The Sprint SP was comparable to the SS, and the Sprint High Sierra was the same as the new El Camino Estate. Sprint literature had more of a "muscle" orientation than did literature for the El Camino.

Late in the 1973 model year, another El Camino trim option was introduced, initially as a "special edition." It was named Conquista, and it came with additional moldings along the front fenders, sides and tailgate, and two-tone paint. The hood and a stripe extending down both sides and around the tailgate were one color; the top of the cab, the upper portion of the truck box and the bottoms of the fenders, doors and tailgate were all painted the second color. A two-page advertisement in the August 1973 issue of *Hot Rod* devoted one page to a picture of the "new special edition El Camino Conquista in the San Gabriel Mountains, California," and, the other page had the heading: "Hightail it. Chevy El Camino. Order a 454 V-8 and take off."

CHAPTER THIRTEEN
1974

This year saw the first major increase in gasoline prices resulting from OPEC actions. Combined El Camino/Sprint sales dropped over twenty percent from the previous model year. Sales literature had all but ignored the word "truck," and (using perfect hindsight) we can say that the vehicle became larger at the wrong time. Length overall was now 216 inches and curb weight for the lightest V-8 was now 3,950 pounds.

Some new names for trim options were instituted. There was still a standard El Camino, but the fancier one was now referred to as the El Camino Classic. The Classic had more trim, both inside and out. In addition, it came with three more options: the SS, the Estate and the Conquista. (The Conquista trim option was to become extremely popular for this and following years.)

Terry Boyce's book on Chevy Super Sports reports that the Super Sport option was on 4,543 of the 1974 models of El Caminos. The SS lines had been dropped from other Chevelle lines at the end of the 1973 model year but continued on the El Camino (to this day). In 1974 the SS option was also available on the

This photo was provided through the courtesy of the Stockland Company of Irvine, California. It shows one of its camper shells on a mid-70's El Camino.

Chevrolet Nova line (where it would continue through 1976).

Ten different vinyl roof colors were available in 1974, and there were sixteen choices of single-color paints. The Conquista option had twenty-one two-tone combinations from which the buyer could choose. In the dealers' data book, the list of available combinations of exterior trim colors and interior decor was now longer and more complicated than the tables which specified all the available drive trains.

This year's "standard" engine was now the 350-ci V-8 with a four-barrel carburetor. A variation, with a four-barrel carburetor, was to be ordered for registration in California. The 400-ci engine was listed as having two variations, one for inside and one for outside California. The 454 option was also available, and could be registered in California. (California sales were especially important since, in some years, three quarters of all El Camino sales were in the area of Denver and west.)

The Turbo Hydra-matic was available with all the El Camino engines. A three-speed shift could be obtained with the 350-ci engine, and a four-speed close-ratio was available for coupling with the 454. (This year the sales literature and dealers' data book made no reference to horsepower.) Tire size was G78-14/B on all El Caminos except the SS, which came on G70-14/B's.

This year's Sprint was available in a standard model, a Classic, the SP and the High Sierra. Sprint literature showed a vehicle with trim similar to that of the Conquista, but made no special mention of the specific trim. The literature said: "Sprint now comes in a range of available models attuned to every taste. Sprint Classic offers a balanced approach to function and style; Sprint High Sierra provides the polished look of an estate vehicle and Sprint SP, in combination with available engines and transmissions, offers the excitement of a well tuned chassis and suspension system that were made for the open road."

An all-black model with vinyl top and rear side rails. This has been customized to the extent that the El Camino nameplates have been removed.

The 1974 with Conquista trim. *(Chevrolet)*

The 1974 SS. *(Chevrolet)*

The wood-grained Estate trim, used on both El Caminos and Sprints.

The canvas cover is held on by snaps. This El Camino Classic has two-tone Conquista paint option—the wide stripe around the sides and rear.

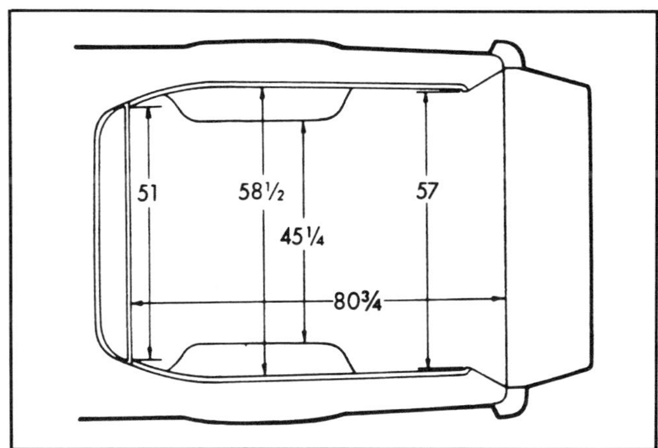

The 1973 through 1977 El Caminos had this box. *(Chevrolet)*

A 1974 Sprint with the wood-grain trim. This photo was originally used as part of a press release. *(National Automotive History Collection, Detroit Public Library)*

CHAPTER FOURTEEN
1975

Once again a six-cylinder engine was available for El Caminos, no doubt reflecting buyers' concern for fuel economy. The 250-ci L6 was advertised as "new" and "designed to meet today's need for economy. . . ." It had a single-barrel carburetor, was rated at 105 net hp, and came with either a three-speed transmission or Turbo Hydra-matic. The 350 came in two versions: with a two-barrel carburetor, rated at 145 net hp (and unavailable in California); and with a four-barrel carburetor, rated at 155 net hp. Both of the 350's came with the same transmission choices as the L6. Also offered were a 400-ci with 175 net hp, and a 454 with 215 net hp (which couldn't be registered in California). These last two engines both had four-barrel carburetors and came with Turbo Hydra-matic only. Hence, only two transmissions were offered for El Caminos this year, the smallest number since El Caminos had been introduced. The standard tire was now GR78-15/B, except for the SS, which used GR70-15/B's.

El Camino literature also pictured an SS with a camper shell which "protects your cargo from the weather, or gives you the makings of a mini-camper."

This 1975 Classic has special striping. The camper shell was by Glasstite of Dunnell, Minnesota.

The literature also indicated that these shells were a dealer-installed accessory, the first time such reference had been made, although literature for earlier years sometimes showed several El Caminos with one in the background fitted with a camper shell. Sprint literature for 1975 also featured a picture of the Sprint with a camper shell. This new thinking may reflect the de-emphasis on the El Camino as a muscle car as well as recognition of the fact that many El Camino owners were using camper shells. (One Chevrolet official said that, in some years, Los Angeles Chevrolet dealers used "free" camper shells as an inducement to prospective El Camino buyers.)

The El Caminos for 1975 came in a standard and a Classic model. Three Classic options were the SS, the Estate and the Conquista which were unchanged from the previous year. The GMC Sprint came in standard and a Classic version with the latter having three options: SP, High Sierra and Sierra Madre del Sur (comparable to the El Camino Classic Conquista).

This was a lousy year for sales. SS production dropped to 3,521 units. Combined El Camino/Sprint 1975 models accounted for only 36,671 units, the lowest since 1967. Sprint's share of that small pie was only 8.3 percent, and this was—and continues to be—its all-time low in both number of units and share of combined El Camino/Sprint total sales.

A general aviation airport was the setting for this photo used as the cover on 1975 literature. *(Harrah's Automobile Collection)*

The GMC Sprint for 1975 was designed for the person who wanted a combination of excitement and comfort.

On moving days, it's nice to have an El Camino owner for a friend.

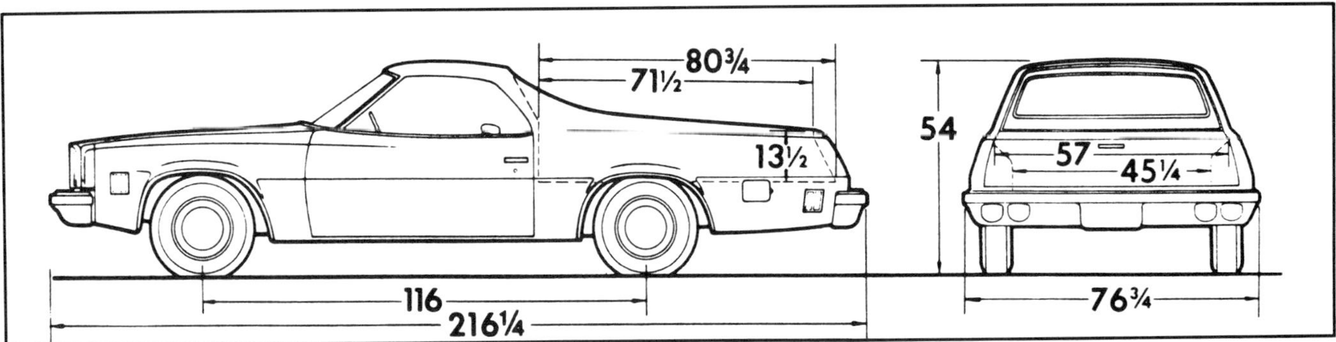

The 1975 El Camino. El Caminos from 1973 through 1977 had similar and approximately the same dimensions. Overall length on the 1976 and 1977 models was 213.25 inches. *(Chevrolet)*

Two of the optional seats for the 1975 Sprint were pictured in this sales brochure. *(GMC)*

John M. Yates, of Indiana, is shown standing by his 1975 El Camino Classic. He's wearing an El Camino T-shirt and a Chevy belt buckle. His El Camino has been heavily customized. The view inside the opened left door shows van seats and carpeting. The opening below the first aid kit was on many El Caminos and leads to a compartment under the front of the truck bed. Stereo speakers are in the two side doors. Additional speakers are on either side of the TV screen in the back. The window at the rear of the cab has been removed. *(John M. Yates)*

This 1975 El Camino Classic belongs to Sherm Mehlhoff of California. It has been lowered five inches in the front and four in the rear, and suspension set up for high-speed cornering. It has a 350 engine. Color is orange-metallic with tan vinyl top. *(Sherm Mehlhoff)*

At the Mill Valley flea market.

CHAPTER FIFTEEN
1976

Sales recovered for 1976 models. El Camino sales were up thirty-four percent and Sprint sales were up by seventy-eight percent. Their combined total—50,326 units—represented an increase of thirty-seven percent over sales of 1975 models. El Camino SS sales did even better, increasing by forty-seven percent to 5,163 units!

The standard powerplants were the 250-ci L6 (rated at 105 net hp) and the new 305-ci V-8 (rated at 140 net hp). However, the latter could not be registered in California. Optional V-8's were a 350 rated at 145 net hp and unavailable for registration in California; another version of the same engine with a four-barrel carburetor and a 165-net-hp rating; and a 400-ci with four-barrel carburetor and a 175-net-hp rating. The six came with a three-speed manual transmission and an option of Turbo Hydra-matic. The V-8's came with Turbo Hydra-matic only. Note that the 454 had been dropped.

Four headlights came on the 1976 El Camino Classics, the first use of four headlights on El Caminos since 1970 models. However, standard 1976 El Caminos had only one headlight on each side, and

The GMC Sprint with this trim option was referred to as the Sierra Madre del Sur. *(GMC)*

were very close in appearance to all 1975 models. Overall vehicle length was 213 inches, three inches less than in 1974 and 1975. Sales literature for El Caminos again showed camper shells and indicated that both shells and tonneau covers were available as dealer-installed options.

While the power train options were being reduced in number, there seemed to be no end to the trim options available. The 1976 dealers' data book dealt extensively with the great number of color possibilities available. Besides the El Camino classics Conquista option there was also the SS which came without side moldings and had a wide painted stripe on each side, extending from the front of the front door rearward. The letters "SS" were painted in front of the molding and also as a grille emblem. One trim option had been dropped this year. It was the Classic Estate which had had the vinyl "wood-grain" along the sides.

Sprints came in a standard version (with single headlights) and in a Classic version (with double headlights). Two trim options on the Sprint Classic were the Sierra Madre del Sur (similar to the El Camino Classic) and the SP (similar to the SS). The Sprint Classic Estate was no longer available.

This drawing from a 1976 dealers' manual shows the Conquista paint option, as offered on the 1974-1977 models. *(Chevrolet)*

On the 1973-77 models the rear body sloped downward, which had to be compensated for by the builders of camper shells. This is illustrated by the shape of the dark triangle.

A 1976 GMC Sprint Classic. Close-up shot shows nameplate which appears behind side doors.

El Camino Classic with camper body going through a Cub Scout car wash in Saco, Maine.

A 1976 GMC Sprint Classic.

This 1976 El Camino Classic belongs to Todd A. Martin of New York. Most noticeable custom features are roll bar with fog lights. Fog light covers have Chevrolet emblem. The grille has been painted burgundy to match striping on sides. In side view of rear, note striping carried over cab. Vehicle has stereo, CB radio and a radar detector. *(Todd Martin)*

A 1976 El Camino Classic.

CHAPTER SIXTEEN
1977

This was to be the last year for the El Camino design which had been introduced in 1973. In the interim, much had happened to the auto industry and to the motoring public. While the 1973 El Camino came with no six-cylinder engines and a choice of four V-8's, by 1977 the selection had been reduced to one L6 and two V-8's, with the largest being a 350-ci, compared with a 454-ci in 1973. This would be the last large El Camino; the term "downsizing" was used throughout the industry, and the following year's El Camino would be smaller.

The six-cylinder engine offered in 1977 had 110 net hp with 250 cubic inches (although when outfitted for registration in California, this engine was rated at only 90 net hp). A 305-ci V-8, which could not be registered in California, was rated at 145 net hp. The 350 V-8 had a 270-net-hp rating (except when outfitted for California, when its rating was 260). All V-8's came with Turbo Hydra-matic. Six-cylinder buyers had the choice between that transmission and the standard three-speed manual. Note that only three engine options were available (in California, only two). Recall

This 1977 El Camino Classic has a Gem Top body. *(Gem Top)*

that in some earlier years there were as many as eight different engines from which to choose.

The standard El Camino in 1977 came with one pair of headlights while the Classic had two pairs. The Classic continued to have two additional trim options, the Conquista and the SS.

Sprints came in standard and Classic models, with two additional trims available on the latter: Sierra Madre del Sur and SP. This was the last year the vehicle would be named Sprint.

Despite all of this, sales were high for 1977 models. The combined El Camino/Sprint sales were 60,276, the highest since 1973 and the third highest since the El Camino had been introduced in the late 1950's. El Camino SS sales were 5,226 units, virtually the same as for 1976.

Perhaps the U.S. buyer was becoming acclimated to paying sixty cents for a gallon of gasoline. At about this time, I was serving as a consultant to the staff of the National Transportation Policy Study Commission in Washington, D.C., and one of the theories bandied about there concerning the increased popularity of light trucks and vans was that the shrinking size of automobiles made the trucks a more popular choice for individuals who wanted both automobile comfort and the occasional ability to carry large loads.

This custom grille, adaptable to El Caminos and Sprints of the mid-'70's, is sold by Stull Industries, Inc., of Buena Park, California. *(Stull Industries, Inc.)*

Side rails and special lettering dress up this El Camino with the Conquista trim

Rear view of a 1977 GMC Sprint.

A 1977 El Camino with Conquista trim option.

A 1977 GMC Sprint.

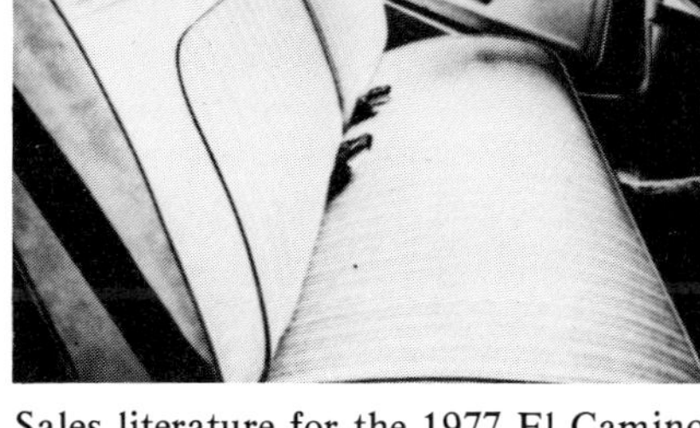

Sales literature for the 1977 El Camino illustrates three interior choices. The top shows a fold-down center armrest; the center, swing bucket seats; and bottom, the standard bench seat. *(Chevrolet)*

A 1977 El Camino SS.

This '77 has a grille of its own. Lettering says Malibu Classic.

A 1977 El Camino Classic with new sport wheel covers and the Conquista trim which included two colors of paint and extra body moldings.

CHAPTER SEVENTEEN
1978

This year's El Camino sported a completely new and downsized body. However, its wheelbase was not shortened by as much as the wheelbase for comparable Chevys; indeed, the new wheelbase, 117 inches, was one inch longer than on the 1973-77 models. The vehicle's total weight had been reduced from 3,752 pounds to 3,174 pounds, and its overall length had been reduced by one foot! For the first time, the El Camino had a unique chassis—it was shared with no other Chevrolet. (Front end sheet metal was shared with the Malibu and side doors with the Monte Carlo.) Weight-carrying capability was unchanged and the interior dimensions of the cargo box remained about the same, although the front corners, rather than being square, had curved contours. (I was told—but was unable to verify the statement—that at least one camper shell manufacturer stopped building shells for El Caminos at this time because of difficulties in designing and manufacturing a body that could fit snugly into the new El Camino bed.) The license plate holder was recessed into the rear tailgate.

The cab now had a small, rear quarter window, which added to its rakish appearance. The rear win-

The "standard El Camino Classic" for 1978 was the lowest-priced model offered that year.

dow glass was curved. The spare tire was stored flat, under the truck bed, in a compartment, which stretched the width of the cab, behind the front seat. A spare tire "extractor" was included.

Steve Thompson, writing in the April 1978 issue of *Car and Driver* said, after driving a 1978 El Camino with the 350-ci V-8 with Turbo Hydra-matic: ". . . once you've hammered some astounded Z-car driver in an on-ramp race you'll never think of it [the El Camino] as a Saturday-afternoon fertilizer hauler again." Thompson's El Camino "managed to knock off consistent sub-nine-second 0-60 runs, and stop the quarter-mile clocks at 17.2 seconds and 82 mph." His top speed was 112 mph.

Wheel size was now 14x6 and the standard tire was P205/75R-14.

Some minor changes in model nomenclature took place. The dealers' data book refers to only two models, the Classic and the Super Sport (SS). The Conquista trim could be ordered with the Classic. During the model year, another trim option, the Royal Knight, would be offered. It was an all-black El Camino with a large decal on the top of the hood. The Super Sport had an air dam below the front bumper, and the air dam and lower panels extending around the vehicle were painted a different color than the top. On the lower panel of each side door was large block lettering spelling "Super Sport."

There was little apparent difference in the interior trims or trim options offered for any of the 1978 El Caminos. As for exteriors, the standard Classic came with the choice of fourteen paint colors and the option of seven vinyl roof colors. The Conquista came in twelve two-tone combinations, and the Super Sport was available in twenty different color combinations and, in addition, the large lettering on the side was available in red, black, gold or blue.

Engines available for registration outside California were a new 200-ci V-6, rated at 95 net hp; a 305 V-8 rated at 145; and a 350 V-8 rated at 170. California engines were a new 231-ci V-6 with 105 net hp; the 305 V-8 with a 135 rating; and the 305 V-8 with a 160 rating. The engines available for registration in California came with automatic transmission only. The El Caminos that could be registered outside California came with a choice between automatic and manual

The 1978 interiors were roomy and nicely styled. A new energy-absorbing padded instrument panel featured a rectangular instrument cluster. Seat had a full-foam padded cushion and backrest.

This Conquista has side rails on the cargo box. *(Chevrolet)*

This black El Camino has a matching black tonneau cover.

This hood decal, introduced in 1978, was part of the trim for both the El Camino Royal Knight and the GMC Caballero Diablo. *(Chevrolet)*

transmissions. A three-speed manual came with the V-6, and a four-speed manual was available with the V-8.

The GMC version of the El Camino was renamed the Caballero. The Caballero Laredo came with the El Camino's Conquista trim. A third version, the Diablo, was similar to El Camino's Super Sport. It had the air dam below the grille, painted the same as the second color along the bottom on both sides, and with the word Diablo in large letters at the bottom of each door. The two Diablos pictured in GMC literature issued in a revised form in March of 1978 have the Royal Knight emblem on the hood, but no special mention is made of the emblem in the text.

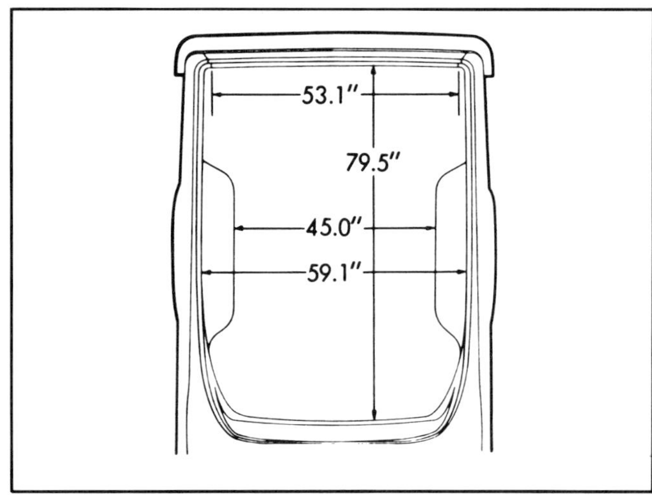

Shape and dimensions of box used on 1978 through 1982 models. Note curved front end. *(Chevrolet)*

Tube behind gas cap leads to air valve for inflating rear shocks.

Bob Wingate drives this 1978 Super Sport and has side lettering to match the style of Super Sport lettering below door. *(Bob Wingate)*

Conquista with two-tone paint.

CHAPTER EIGHTEEN
1979

This would be a good year for El Camino/Caballero sales. The combined total for both for the 1979 model year was 64,960 units, a figure which was second highest for all time. Albert Olson, Jr., Chevrolet's assistant general sales manager, said that El Camino sales were high at this time because the six-cylinder engine was relatively fuel-efficient and that buyers were finding the El Camino to be a much more comfortable and attractive vehicle than the Japanese import pickup trucks. (A marketing survey conducted by Chevrolet of a sample of 1979 El Camino buyers found that ninety percent of them said they would have purchased a light-duty truck if the El Camino had not been available.)

Interestingly, the only other year for which sales were higher was in 1973. Hence, both peaks were reached on the eve of major increases in the price of gasoline.

This year's El Camino came in two models, a standard one and the Super Sport. The trim option on the standard was the Conquista two-tone paint. The option on the Super Sport was the Royal Knight trim, which came in nine solid colors with matching rally

The Super Sport for 1979. Note air dam under front bumper. *(Chevrolet)*

wheels, and had narrow striping on the sides and tailgate and a huge decal on top of the hood. Both the Royal Knight and Super Sport had an air dam in front that was painted the same color as the body (in the case of the Super Sport, the air dam and the rally wheels were the same color as the lower trim).

Two engines were available for California registration, a 231-ci V-6 rated at 115 net hp; and the 305 V-8, rated at 155 net hp. Both came coupled with an automatic transmission only.

Four engines were available for registration outside California. The 200-ci V-6 was rated at 94 net hp and came with a three-speed manual transmission or an automatic. The 267 V-8 was rated at 125 net hp and came with either a four-speed manual or an automatic transmission. The 305 V-8 was rated at 160 hp and had the same transmission choices as the 267. (Literature referred to both the 267 and 305 as "new.") The 350 V-8 was rated at 165 net hp and was coupled with an automatic transmission.

One form of option, about which little has been said to this point, was radios and other sound systems. The variety of equipment offered this year apparently peaked, reflecting the great interest in CB radios. Here, from the dealers' data book, is the listing of radio equipment options and their 1979 prices.

AM radio $85
AM/FM radio $158
AM/FM stereo radio $232
AM radio with 8-track stereo tape system $248
AM/FM stereo radio with 8-track stereo tape system $335
AM-FM stereo radio with stereo cassette tape $341
AM-FM/Citizens Band radio with power antenna $489
AM-FM stereo/Citizens Band radio with power antenna $570
AM-FM stereo radio with digital clock display $395
Dual front speakers (included with some systems and optional with others) $21
Windshield antenna $27
Power antenna $47

GMC Caballero sales were the highest in the Sprint/Caballero history. The standard Caballero was comparable to the standard El Camino. The Caballero Laredo was comparable to the standard El Camino

This 1979 not only has the standard grille but also the air dam which came only with Super Sports and Royal Knights.

A closer view of the side windows on the 1979 model.

This El Camino has a special grille and smoked light covers. *(Steve Stefinsky)*

New for 1979 was the Super Sport with the Royal Knight option with special striping and a hood decal. *(Chevrolet)*

with Conquista trim; and the Caballero Diablo was comparable to the El Camino Super Sport with the Royal Knight's sizzling flame decal on its hood.

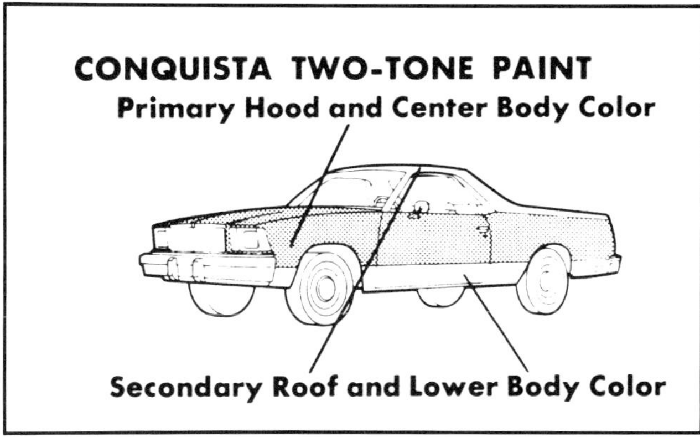

The Conquista paint option on 1978-82 models. *(Chevrolet)*

The 1979 Royal Knight. *(Chevrolet)*

A side view of the 1979 with the Conquista trim. *(Chevrolet)*

The standard El Camino for 1979.

CHAPTER NINETEEN
1980

Sales were poor in 1980 for the entire industry, in part because of the large price increases for retail gasoline. El Camino/Caballero sales for the model year dropped to 45,674 units, the lowest since 1975.

There were very few changes from the previous year's models. For California registration, the same two engines as were available for 1979 were offered, although the V-6 was now rated at 100 net hp. For registration outside California, the smallest engine was now a 229-ci V-6 which was rated at 115 net hp and came with a three-speed manual or an automatic shift. Also available, and with automatic transmission only, was the 267-ci V-8 rated at 120 net hp. The 305 V-8 was rated at 155 and came with either a four-speed manual or an automatic transmission.

The following are Chevrolet Division's suggested 1980 retail prices (exclusive of destination charges):
Standard El Camino $5,703
Conquista trim $165
El Camino Super Sport $5,934
Royal Knight trim $73
267-ci V-8 $80
305-ci V-8 $195

The 1980 GMC Caballero with the Laredo trim option. *(GMC)*

Air conditioning $601
Clock, electric $25
Console (available when bucket seats were ordered) $86
Cooling, heavy-duty $36 or $63
Cover, cargo box tonneau $116
Door locks, power $93
Gauge package, including voltmeter, temperature, oil pressure, tachometer $134
Glass, tinted $75
Moldings, body side $57
Radio equipment (similar to 1979) $97-525
Rails, cargo box side $79
Roof cover, vinyl $81
Seat, six-way power $175
Seats and trim
- cloth buckets $91
- cloth 50/50 $184
- vinyl bench $28
- vinyl buckets $91
- vinyl 50/50 $212

Speed control $112
Steering, power $174
Tank, 22-gallon fuel (in place of 17.7-gallon standard equipment) $23
Tie-downs, for cargo box $20
Transmission, automatic $358
Transmission, four-speed manual $144
Wheel covers, sport silver or sport gold $56
Wheel covers, wire $125
Wheels, rally $50
Windows, power $143
Windshield wipers, intermittent $41

The 1980 dealers' data book showed the many trim combinations available for the standard El Camino, the Conquista, the Super Sport, and the Royal Knight.

There was little change in the Caballero offerings for 1980. It came in the standard, Laredo and Diablo versions. Note the pattern of having three offerings, while the El Camino has four (the standard, Conquista, Super Sport and Royal Knight).

For 1980 interiors were color-keyed to the outside paint to give a coordinated look. Standard interior was available with a vinyl trimmed bench seat; shown here are the optional buckets and console.

Two-tone trim combination. *(Chevrolet)*

Seat and shoulder belts were also color-coordinated in 1980 interiors. Seats came in either vinyl or cloth (shown).

Rear view of a 1980 Royal Knight. Snaps are for canvas cover.

The grille and the fence have similar patterns.

Dash and instrument panel for 1980 included many accessories: air conditioning; Comfortilt steering wheel; special gauge package including voltmeter, temperature, oil pressure and tachometer; electric door locks and electric power windows.

This camper shell, with the trade name Voyager, is much higher at the rear than at the front. Note size of rear window.

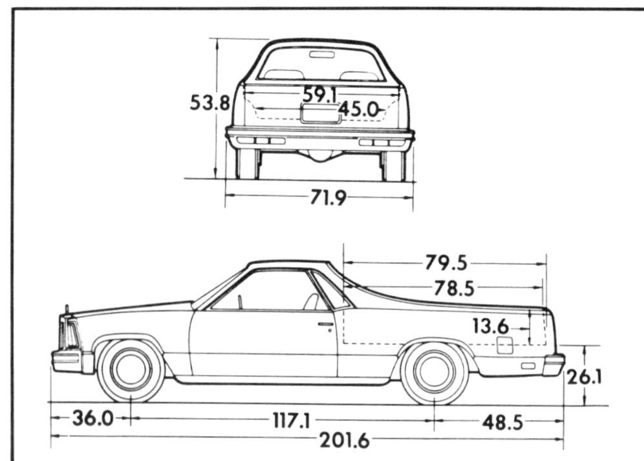

El Caminos from 1978 through 1982 had the same dimensions as shown here for this 1980 model. *(Chevrolet)*

CHAPTER TWENTY
1981

This was another model which reflected few changes. The two powerplants available in 1981 for California registration were the 231-ci V-6, rated at 110 net hp; and the 305 V-8, rated at 145. Both came with the automatic transmission only. Outside California, three engines were available. The 229-ci V-6 was rated at 110 net hp and came with the choice of a three-speed manual or an automatic shift. The 267 V-8 came with an automatic transmission only, and was rated at 115. The 305 V-8 came with either a four-speed manual or an automatic transmission and had a 145-net-hp rating.

The standard El Camino came with the Conquista trim option which included: bright-metal moldings on the front fenders, body sides and tailgate (to serve as a "break" between the two colors of paint); the word Conquista inside above the glove compartment door, and outside at the right top of the tailgate.

The Super Sport had a front air dam, which was painted the lower body color; twin sport side mirrors; Super Sport decals along the bottom of both doors and on the tailgate; black quarter-window moldings; a second color of paint along the bottom; rally

The 1981 Caballero Amarillo with two-tone paint. *(GMC)*

wheels; and the words Super Sport inside above the glove compartment. The Royal Knight option for the Super Sport was a single color, and had the large hood decal, narrow striping along the sides and on the tailgate, and the Royal Knight decal on the sides and tailgate.

Trim options were reduced in number. The standard El Camino came in fourteen single colors, and with no two-tone combinations. The Super Sport came with nine color choices for the upper portion which could be combined with various lower panel accent colors for a total of fifteen combinations. The Conquista trim also came in fifteen two-tone combinations, and the Royal Knight came in a choice of nine solid colors for the body and three colors for the decals. Vinyl roofs were no longer listed as available. One new feature was the 55/45 seat (with forty-five percent being on the driver's side, and with an armrest).

The GMC Caballero came in a standard version, the model with the El Camino's Conquista trim was now called the Caballero Amarillo. (Formerly the model had been called Laredo; both are cities in Texas.) The Caballero Diablo was comparable to the Royal Knight.

Literature for both the Caballero and the El Camino made reference to computer-controlled emission systems. Caballero literature said: "All 1981 engines for the GMC Caballero are equipped with this exciting new computer-controlled system that reduces Caballero's emissions to the lowest level in GMC history. Space-age technology employs an on-board computer, an oxygen sensor, other engine sensors, and an electromechanical fuel metering system in the carburetor to control the ratio of fuel/air induction. The system is also engineered so the engine will continue to function in the event of a computer malfunction."

Sales for 1981 El Caminos and Caballeros were low, totaling just over 41,000 units, the lowest since 1975.

All seats, including the standard split-back bench seat (bottom left), were trimmed with fabrics for 1981. The new optional 55/45 split seat (top) and the optional bucket seats (bottom right) as well as the standard bench were accompanied by new, convenient pull straps on the doors.

Camper shell is by Olympic Body of Elkhart, Indiana. Photo was taken in Cambridge, Massachusetts.

The Conquista trim option with dark stripe around bottom and on top including the roof. Close-up shows curved front end of box and cargo tie-downs.

The camper shell's roof is parallel to the top of the box and slopes downward to the rear. This El Camino was parked on the grounds of the Minnesota State Fair.

CHAPTER TWENTY-ONE
1982

One obvious change in this year's El Caminos and Caballeros was the use of four headlights in the front. The same body as had been in use since 1978 continued.

There was little change in powerplants offered except that the 305-ci V-8 (in both the California and non-California versions) was now rated at 150 net hp. The automatic transmission came as standard equipment this year.

The El Camino continued to come in four versions: the standard, the standard with Conquista trim, the Super Sport and the Super Sport with the Royal Knight trim. The number of available colors and color combinations continued to decline. The standard El Camino came in eleven single colors only. The Conquista came in only eight two-tone combinations while the Super Sport came with only seven. The Royal Knight came with seven solid colors and three decal colors.

The 1982 GMC version came in three models: the standard Caballero, the Diablo and the Amarillo.

It is anticipated that 1983 El Caminos and Caballeros will continue with the same chassis and body design.

El Camino Conquista in Redwood Metallic and Beige
El Camino Super Sport in White and Lt. Brown Metallic
El Camino Super Sport in Silver Metallic and Dk. Blue Metallic
El Camino in Dk. Jade Metallic
El Camino Conquista in Dk. Blue Metallic and White
El Camino Royal Knight in Redwood Metallic

Variety of El Camino models for 1982.

This PR photo shows the 1982 Caballero, featuring the new grille styling, with a camping trailer. *(GMC)*

For 1982, El Camino offered a wealth of interior options; from the standard interior to the optional 45/55 split seat to the special custom interior with knit velour upholstery shown here.

Included in the 1982 option list was the large front air dam as shown here.

New instrument panel with steering-column-mounted fingertip control switch.

LITERATURE, ADS, PHOTOS

Separate literature pieces were issued for El Caminos (and for Sprints and Caballeros) each year. There is one apparent exception: In 1960, the same piece of literature described both the El Camino and the sedan delivery. For a few model years, there was some reference on the literature's front cover indicating that one was looking at "truck" literature. (Early in my work on this book, I visited the library of Harrah's Automobile Collection and discovered that for about half of the model years, the librarian had filed the El Camino brochures under "Chevrolet Autos," and the other half, under "Chevrolet Trucks.")

GMC Sprint literature appeared in 1971. The GMC literature used its own artwork, although often the same feature would be pictured in both the El Camino and Sprint brochures, but slightly different photos or line drawings would be used. Sprint literature was more likely to have a reference to trucks on the cover. Sprint literature was often only four pages while El Camino literature was usually six pages. The four-page layout for Sprint literature may have been to ensure compatibility with other GMC truck literature and allow placement in binders. Beginning in

NEW
CHEVROLET
EL CAMINO!

Good looks never carried so much weight!

Look at those lines . . . and that load space! El Camino combines the crisp new Slimline design of the '59 Chevrolet passenger car with a spacious, sturdy pickup box. It's the sportiest load carrier that ever took to the road. Rides and handles like a convertible with its quick, smooth response. Has a finish that needs no wax or polish for up to three years. Yet it hauls and hustles like the workingest thing on wheels.

You can have V8 or new Hi-Thrift 6 power. And there's a choice of four transmissions, including smoother-than-ever Turboglide as an extra-cost option. On the business end of El Camino you find a sturdy, full-width pickup box and solid, ribbed-steel load platform. El Camino is ready to do a man-size job of carrying cargo—over a thousand pounds of it. In fact, with its dual personality, El Camino is ready for just about anything. It serves as a sure prestige builder for businesses, as an extra-handy helper for do-it-yourselfers, and it's a natural for outdoor sportsmen. Stop by your Chevrolet dealer's one of these days soon and look over El Camino. . . . Chevrolet Division of General Motors, Detroit 2, Michigan.

CHEVROLET

Large full-page ad for first year of El Camino.

Only El Camino could lead so many lives

CHEVROLET
EL CAMINO

Only El Camino could look so much at home in so many different settings. It works, for example, with the weight-carrying ability of a half-ton truck. After hours, it provides all the dash of a Chevy passenger car, including a quieter, more comfortable ride than you'll find in most passenger cars. Picture a Camino winding up into the Sierras loaded with camping gear. (Great!) Or off for La Jolla with long, sleek surfboards in the box. See what we mean? For work or sport or even major do-it-yourself projects, or for all three—nothing on four wheels fills the bill so beautifully. Think about it. . . . Chevrolet Division of General Motors, Detroit 2, Michigan.

This ad for 1960 El Caminos originally appeared in *Sunset*, a magazine with mostly Western readership. The geographic references in the ad are aimed at the Los Angeles/Southern California market.

1978, GMC literature was for the Caballero, and in 1979 the GMC literature piece increased to six pages, although trimmed and folded so that it still could be placed in a three-ring binder. This continued in 1980 when an interesting sentence was added toward the end of the brochure: "This vehicle is also available from Chevrolet dealers under the name Chevrolet El Camino." El Camino literature for the previous year (1979) had contained a similar reference to Caballeros. One can ponder why this cross-reference was included.

El Camino and Sprint/Caballero restorers can obtain a fairly good idea of what their vehicle should look like by buying some original literature from dealers, at flea markets or through advertisements in old car enthusiasts' magazines. In 1981, prices for a single year's literature ranged from ten dollars (for the oldest) down to about three dollars for recent years. (In some model years, revised literature was issued in mid-year, apparently to include new trim options which had become available.)

Auto historians Howard and Shelby Applegate wrote a thoughtful article in the February 1980 issue of *Car Exchange* which traced the evolution and development of El Caminos and Sprint/Caballeros. As their only apparent source of information they used the literature for each year. They traced the changes in specifications and models and, more importantly, they attempted to interpret the message of the advertising theme in each year's brochure to determine the market at which the message was aimed. They conclude: "This is the age of 'do your own thing,' 'create your own space,' the gusto age. The El Camino literature reflects this urge to enjoy life, even while you're working and encourages the current need to make a personal statement of lifestyle."

The El Camino was, of course, advertised. Bill Franson, of San Diego, supplied me with a wide sampling of magazine advertisements. Reproduced here are several which deal with the El Camino's dual personality. Other ads sometimes pictured a size range of Chevrolet trucks, with the El Camino being one of the smallest—and certainly the sleekest—models.

GMC truck spokesman Chuck Licari said the company did little advertising solely for the Sprint/Caballero because of the vehicle's low sales volume. He

El Camino '66: smarter on the outside...

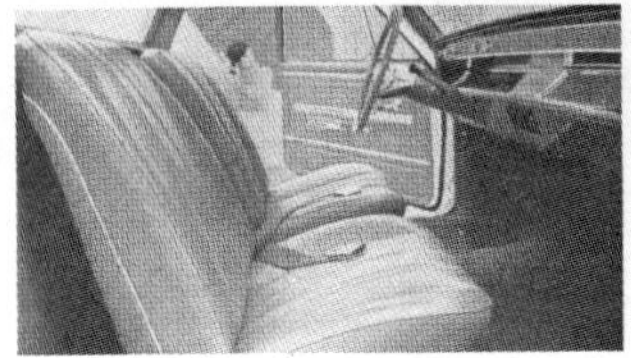

nicer on the inside...

more powerful up front...

and still a downright pleasure to work with!

More than ever, El Camino offers the appearance, comfort and performance of a spirited passenger car. Yet it remains ideally suited to work as a service or towing vehicle. We offer it for '66 as an even more unique answer to the special requirements of enthusiasts.

Here's what we did to make a good thing even better: restyled the exterior from grille to tail lights and added six new colors to the paint chart; also, redesigned the instrument panel, steering wheel, door panels and upholstery—made the cab more stylish and practical than ever.

As for power teams—we expanded the choice of engine/transmission combinations so that now there are 23 different ways to go. The selection includes two Sixes and five V8's—the newest of which is a 396 cubic-incher—along with 3-speed, 4-speed and Powerglide automatic transmissions.

Yet, for all these changes, El Camino still features a roomy six-foot pickup box, over a thousand pounds of payload capacity, and the inherent ride smoothness of a four-wheel coil spring suspension and load-leveler shocks.

All that's lacking now is you behind the wheel—and you can fix that at your Chevrolet dealer's. . . . Chevrolet Division of General Motors, Detroit, Michigan.

New El Camino by CHEVROLET

This ad appeared in *Motor Trend.* The text made reference to the El Camino's use "as a service or towing vehicle."

Chevy El Camino.
A car when you need a car.
A truck when you need a truck.

On the town: El Camino offers passenger-car good looks, luxury interiors in a wide selection of fabrics and colors and Full Coil suspension ride. Passenger-car performance, too. A 305* V8 with a wide range of job applications is standard on V8 models. A 250 Six and two bigger V8s also available.

On the job: This is a tough truck. It can move up to 800 pounds in the double-walled cargo box (plus as much as 450 pounds of passengers up front). Other double-walled sections include doors, roof, hood and fenders. Air-adjustable rear shock absorbers are standard and help level the ride and the load.

Nice for any occasion: An interior like the El Camino Classic—full-width custom seat with a fold-down center armrest, padded instrument panel, special door panel trim, deluxe vinyl-coated headliner and black-finished rearview mirror. Swivel bucket seats also available.

*Not available in California

YOUR MONEY'S WORTH.
MILE AFTER MILE AFTER MILE.

The city/country theme is in this ad for the 1976 El Camino, which appeared in *Western Outdoors.*

said that it was included in pictures of the entire GMC truck fleet.

It's difficult to say how readily available are factory photographs. Applegate and Applegate list a few El Camino photos in one of their catalogs. Since few dealers list their entire photograph stock at one time, it might be best to make contact with specific queries about El Camino or Sprint/Caballero photos. There are, of course, many El Caminos on the streets which can be photographed. Virtually all of the uncredited photos in this book were taken by me in 1981.

Literature for 1960 dealt with both the El Camino and the sedan delivery.

Economy was stressed in this ad for a sporty model.

The Caballero Diablo is pictured at the top of the cover on this 1978 GMC literature.

MODELS

Models of autos and trucks fall into two categories: kits and "promos" (the nickname for promotional material). Most are of plastic and are at about 1/25 scale.

Kits are sold in toy stores and hobby shops. Dennis Doty, author of *The Complete Book of Model Car Building,* kindly supplied a picture of one of his many El Camino kits.

Promos are built for sale to auto dealers who may (or may not) hand them out to good sales prospects. At one time, promos came in all of the same colors as did the full-size car, and one of their functions was to show prospective buyers what different colors would look like.

Unfortunately, El Camino promos were not built for certain years, especially during most of the 1970's. Rob Cerame, who collects promos, graciously supplied me with a photo of one from his El Camino "fleet."

When asked about any relationships between kits and promos, Cerame said: "Kits in hobby shops are basically built from promotional molds but many separate parts and added features are included."

This 1977 Revell kit included a Mini-Trail Bike, an opening hood and "Zoomie" exhaust pipes. *(Revell)*

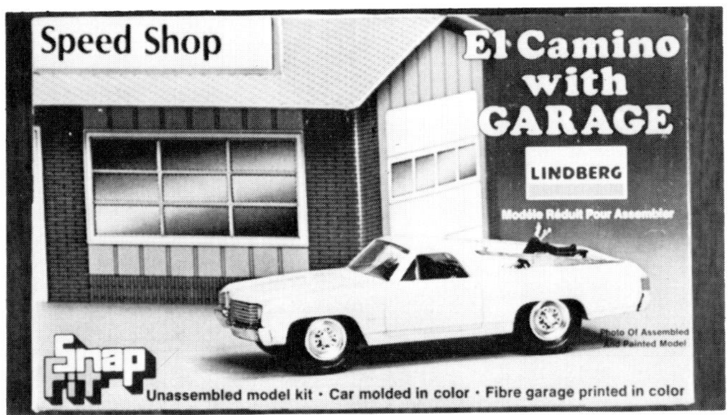

This El Camino kit comes with a garage for the finished model. *(Lindberg Products, Inc.)*

Two Lindberg 1/32 scale model kits of the 1974 El Camino. Both kits also came with a model cycle. *(Dennis Doty)*

Robert Cerame, of Florida, collects promos and he took this shot. *(Robert Cerame)*

APPENDIX

EL CAMINO, GMC SPRINT AND CABALLERO SALES
by model year

Model Year	Chevrolet El Camino	GMC Sprint	GMC Caballero	Total	Sprint/ Caballero Percent of total
1959	22,246			22,246	
1960	14,163			14,163	
1961-1963 no El Camino models					
1964	36,615			36,615	
1965	36,316			36,316	
1966	35,119			35,119	
1967	34,830			34,830	
1968	41,791			41,791	
1969	48,385			48,385	
1970	47,707			47,707	
1971	41,606	3,963		45,569	8.7
1972	57,147	6,492		63,639	10.2
1973	64,987	6,766		71,753	9.4
1974	51,223	4,873		56,096	8.7
1975	33,620	3,051		36,671	8.3
1976	44,890	5,436		50,326	10.8
1977	54,321	5,955		60,276	9.9
1978	54,286		6,609	60,895	10.9
1979	58,008		6,952	64,960	10.7
1980	40,932		4,742	45,674	10.4
1981	36,711		4,380	41,091	10.7

Source: Chevrolet, and GMC Truck & Coach public relations offices

MORE GREAT READING

The Production Figure Book For U.S. Cars. Reflects the relative rarity of various makes, models, body styles, etc. Softbound, 180 pages.

American Truck Spotter's Guide 1920-1970. 170 makes are covered with over 2,000 illustrations. Softbound, 330 pages.

Pickup and Van Spotter's Guide 1945-1982. Covers 15 U.S. and foreign makes with over 1,200 illustrations, 160 pages, softbound.

The Big "Little GTO" Book. All of these Great Ones by Pontiac are covered—1965-1974. Over 150 great photos, 235 pages. Large format, softbound.

Chevy Super Sports 1961-1976. Exciting story of these hot cars with complete specs and data. 176 pages, 234 illustrations, softbound. Large format.

Son of Muscle Car Mania. 176 pages of more great ads from the 1962-1974 muscle car era. All U.S. makes represented. Softbound, 250 illustrations.

Muscle Car Mania. A collection of advertisements for muscle cars 1964 through 1974. 176 pages, 250 illustrations, softbound.

Fearsome Fords 1959-1973. Over 250 photos of these great cars accompany 182 pages of interesting information. Softbound, large format.

Auto Restoration From Junker to Jewel. Illustrated guide to restoring old cars. 292 pages, 289 illustrations, softbound.

Corvair Affair. The whole Corvair story including styling, mechanicals and the Nader connection. 176 pages, over 140 great illustrations.

Classic Motorbooks Chrysler 300 1955-1961 Photofacts. Over 125 photos accompany lots of info on these cars. Softbound, 80 pages.

Classic Motorbooks Pontiac Trans Am 1969-1973 Photofacts. Over 125 great photos help tell the story. 80 pages, softbound.

Bob Bondurant on High Performance Driving. World-famous instructor teaches secrets to fast, safe driving. Over 100 illustrations, 144 pages, softbound.

Classic Motorbooks Ford Retractable 1957-1959 Photofacts. Nearly 200 photos help tell this unique story. Softbound, 80 pages.

Illustrated Ferrari Buyer's Guide. Features all street/production cars 1954 through 1980. 176 pages, over 225 photos, softbound.

Illustrated Porsche Buyer's Guide. Covers the 356 through the 944 from 1950 to 1983 with lots of photos. Softbound, 175 pages.

Panteras For The Road. Over 250 illustrations, many in color cover these great cars, 125 pages. In the Survivors Series.

Autocourse. Large-format racing annual. Coverage of each Grand Prix and other major racing events and series. Over 200 pages with lots of color.

Illustrated Corvette Buyer's Guide. Includes 194 photos and lots of info on all these cars 1953-1982. 156 pages, softbound.

Illustrated High Performance Mustang Buyer's Guide. Covers the 1965 GT, the Shelby, through the 1973 Mach 1. Softbound, 250 illustrations, 176 pages.

Illustrated Alfa Romeo Buyer's Guide. The 6C-2500 through the Montreal are covered with over 200 illustrations. 176 pages, softbound.

Illustrated M.G. Buyer's Guide. Features all the models 1924 through 1982. 160 pages, softbound, over 125 illustrations.

Illustrated Lamborghini Buyer's Guide. Details all models from the first V-12-engined 350 GTV through the 1983 LMA models including many specials. 176 pages, over 250 photos, softbound.

Illustrated Austin-Healey Buyer's Guide. The 100 through the 300 through the Jensen-Healey are covered with over 125 great illustrations. Softbound, 136 pages.

How To Restore Your Collector Car. Covers all the major restoration processes in an easy to understand, easy to use format. More than 300 illustrations. Softbound, 320 pages.

Motorbooks International
Publishers & Wholesalers Inc.
Osceola, Wisconsin 54020, USA